DOROTHEE
SOELLE

MODERN SPIRITUAL MASTERS
Robert Ellsberg, Series Editor

Already published:

Dietrich Bonhoeffer (edited by Robert Coles)
Simone Weil (edited by Eric O. Springsted)
Henri Nouwen (edited by Robert A. Jonas)
Pierre Teilhard de Chardin (edited by Ursula King)
Anthony de Mello (edited by William Dych, S.J.)
Charles de Foucauld (edited by Robert Ellsberg)
Oscar Romero (by Marie Dennis, Rennie Golden,
  and Scott Wright)
Eberhard Arnold (edited by Johann Christoph Arnold)
Thomas Merton (edited by Christine M. Bochen)
Thich Nhat Hanh (edited by Robert Ellsberg)
Rufus Jones (edited by Kerry Walters)
Mother Teresa (edited by Jean Maalouf)
Edith Stein (edited by John Sullivan, O.C.D.)
John Main (edited by Laurence Freeman)
Mohandas Gandhi (edited by John Dear)
Mother Maria Skobtsova (introduction by Jim Forest)
Evelyn Underhill (edited by Emilie Griffin)
St. Thérèse of Lisieux (edited by Mary Frohlich)
Flannery O'Connor (edited by Robert Ellsberg)
Clarence Jordan (edited by Joyce Hollyday)
G. K. Chesterton (edited by William Griffin)
Alfred Delp, SJ (introduction by Thomas Merton)
Bede Griffiths (edited by Thomas Matus)
Karl Rahner (edited by Philip Endean)
Sadhu Sundar Singh (edited by Charles E. Moore)
Pedro Arrupe (edited by Kevin F. Burke, S.J.)
Romano Guardini (edited by Robert A. Krieg)
Albert Schweitzer (edited by James Brabazon)
Caryll Houselander (edited by Wendy M. Wright)
Brother Roger of Taizé (edited by Marcello Fidanzio)

DOROTHEE SOELLE

Essential Writings

Selected with an Introduction by

DIANNE L. OLIVER

ORBIS BOOKS

Maryknoll, New York 10545

Founded in 1970, Orbis Books endeavors to publish works that enlighten the mind, nourish the spirit, and challenge the conscience. The publishing arm of the Maryknoll Fathers and Brothers, Orbis seeks to explore the global dimensions of the Christian faith and mission, to invite dialogue with diverse cultures and religious traditions, and to serve the cause of reconciliation and peace. The books published reflect the views of their authors and do not represent the official position of the Maryknoll Society. To learn more about Maryknoll and Orbis Books, please visit our website at www.maryknoll.org.

Grateful acknowledgment is made to the following for permission to use excerpts from works by Dorothee Soelle: Westminster John Knox Press for permission to print selections from *On Earth as in Heaven* © 1993 by Dorothee Soelle, and *Strength of the Weak* © 1984 by Dorothee Soelle; Continuum International Publishing Group for selections from *Thinking about God* © 1990 by Dorothee Soelle; Pilgrim Press (Cleveland) for *Creative Disobedience*, trans. Lawrence W. Denef, xii–xx, copyright © 1995 by Dorothee Soelle; to Hoffman und Campe Verlag (Hamburg, Germany) for selections from *Theology for Skeptics* copyright © 1990 (Minneapolis: Fortress Press, 1995), *Against the Wind* copyright © 1995 (Minneapolis: Fortress Press, 1999), *The Silent Cry,* copyright © 1997 (Minneapolis: Fortress Press, 2001); Kreuz Verlag (Stuttgart, Germany) for selections from *Choosing Life,* copyright © 1980 by Dorothee Soelle (Philadelphia: Fortress Press, 1981), *The Window of Vulnerability,* copyright © 1990 by Dorothee Soelle (Minneapolis: Fortress Press, 1990), *Political Theology,* copyright © 1971 by Dorothee Soelle (Philadelphia: Fortress Press, 1974), *Suffering,* copyright 1973 by Dorothee Soelle (Philadelphia: Fortress Press, 1975); for all other selections, the Estate of Dorothee Soelle. Special thanks to Fulbert Steffensky for his generous cooperation with this project.

Library of Congress Cataloging-in-Publication Data

Sölle, Dorothee.
   [Selections. English. 2006]
   Dorothee Soelle : essential writings / selected with an introduction by Dianne L. Oliver.
      p. cm. – (Modern spiritual masters series)
   ISBN-13: 978-1-57075-640-5 (pbk.)
   1. Theology. I. Oliver, Dianne L., 1963- II. Title. III. Series.
BX4827.S65A25 2006
230′.044 – dc22

                                         2005027948

Contents

Abbreviations

The following abbreviations are used for Dorothee Soelle's key primary works:

AW	*Against the Wind: Memoir of a Radical Christian*
"Between"	"Between Matter and Spirit: Why and in What Sense Must Theology be Materialist?"
CD	*Creative Disobedience*
CL	*Choosing Life*
DBA	*Death by Bread Alone: Texts and Reflections on Religious Experience*
EH	*On Earth as in Heaven: A Liberation Spirituality of Sharing*
"Mysticism"	"Mysticism, Liberation, and the Names of God"
PT	*Political Theology*
"Resistance"	"Resistance: Toward a First World Theology"
RP	*Revolutionary Patience*
SC	*The Silent Cry: Mysticism and Resistance*
SU	*Suffering*
SW	*The Strength of the Weak: Toward a Christian Feminist Identity*

TG   *Thinking about God: An Introduction to*
                Theology

TS   *Theology for Skeptics: Reflections on God*

TWTL   *To Work and to Love: A Theology of Creation*

WL   *Of War and Love*

WV   *The Window of Vulnerability: A Political*
                Spirituality

Full bibliographical information can be found in the following
section, "Soelle's Works in English."

Soelle's Works in English

BOOKS

Soelle, Dorothee. *Christ the Representative: An Essay in Theology after the "Death of God."* Trans. David Lewis from *Stellvertretung: Ein Kapitel Theologie nach dem "Tode Gottes,"* 1965. London: SCM Press, 1967.

Soelle, Dorothee. *The Truth Is Concrete.* Trans. Dinah Livingstone from *Die Wahrheit ist konkret,* 1967. London: Burns and Oates, 1969.

Soelle, Dorothee. *Beyond Mere Obedience.* Trans. Lawrence W. Denef from *Phantasie und Gehorsam: Überlegungen zu einer künftigen christlichen Ethik,* 1968. Minneapolis: Augsburg Publishing House, 1970.

Soelle, Dorothee. *Political Theology.* Trans. with an introduction by John Shelley from *Politische Theologie, Auseinandersetzung mit Rudolf Bultmann,* 1971. Philadelphia: Fortress Press, 1974.

Soelle, Dorothee. *Revolutionary Patience.* Trans. Robert and Rita Kimber from *Die revolutionäre Geduld,* 1974. Maryknoll, NY: Orbis Books, 1974.

Soelle, Dorothee. *Suffering.* Trans. Everett Kalin from *Leiden,* 1973. Philadelphia: Fortress Press, 1975.

Soelle, Dorothee. *Death by Bread Alone: Texts and Reflections on Religious Experience.* Trans. David L. Scheidt from *Die Hinreise: Zur religiösen Erfahrung, Texte und Überlegungen,* 1975. Philadelphia: Fortress Press, 1978.

Soelle, Dorothee. *Choosing Life.* Trans. Margaret Kohl from *Wählt das Leben,* 1980. Philadelphia: Fortress Press, 1981.

Soelle, Dorothee. *Beyond Mere Dialogue: On Being Christian and Socialist.* Detroit: CFS, 1982.

Soelle, Dorothee. *The Arms Race Kills Even without War.* Trans. Gerhard A. Elston from *Aufrüstung tötet auch ohne Krieg,* 1982. Philadelphia: Fortress Press, 1983.

Soelle, Dorothee. *Of War and Love.* Trans. Rita and Robert Kimber from *Im Hause des Menschenfressers: Texte zum Frieden,* 1981. Maryknoll, NY: Orbis Books, 1983.

Soelle, Dorothee. *The Strength of the Weak: Toward a Christian Feminist Identity.* Trans. Robert and Rita Kimber. Philadelphia: The Westminster Press, 1984.

Soelle, Dorothee, with Shirley A. Cloyes. *To Work and to Love: A Theology of Creation.* Philadelphia: Fortress Press, 1984.

Soelle, Dorothee, and Fulbert Steffensky. *Not Just Yes and Amen: Christians with a Cause.* Trans. Rowohlt Taschenbuch Verlag from *Nicht nur Ja und Amen,* 1984. Philadelphia: Fortress Press, 1985.

Soelle, Dorothee, and C. F. Beyers Naudè. *Hope for Faith: A Conversation.* Risk Book Series, WCC Publications. Grand Rapids: Wm. B. Eerdmans, 1986.

Soelle, Dorothee. *Thinking about God: An Introduction to Theology.* Trans. John Bowden from *Gott Denken: Einführung in die Theologie,* 1990. Philadelphia: Trinity Press International, 1990.

Soelle, Dorothee. *The Window of Vulnerability: A Political Spirituality.* Trans. Linda M. Maloney from *Das Fenster der Verwundbarkeit: Theologisch-politische Texte,* 1990. Minneapolis: Fortress Press, 1990.

Soelle, Dorothee. *On Earth as in Heaven: A Liberation Spirituality of Sharing.* Trans. Marc Batko. Louisville, KY: Westminster/John Knox Press, 1993.

Soelle, Dorothee. *Stations of the Cross: A Latin American Pilgrimage.* Trans. Joyce Irwin from *Gott im Müll: Eine andere Entdeckung Latinamerikas,* 1992. Minneapolis: Fortress Press, 1993.

Soelle, Dorothee. *Great Women of the Bible in Art and Literature.* Commentary by Dorothee Soelle. Macon, GA: Mercer University Press, 1994.

Soelle, Dorothee. *Creative Disobedience.* Trans. Lawrence W. Denef from *Phantasie und Gehorsam: Überlegungen zu einer künftigen christlichen Ethik,* 1968. Cleveland: Pilgrim Press, 1995.

Soelle, Dorothee. *Theology for Skeptics: Reflections on God.* Trans. Joyce L. Irwin from *Es muss doch mehr als alles geben: Nachdenken über Gott,* 1992. Minneapolis: Fortress Press, 1995.

Soelle, Dorothee. *Against the Wind: Memoir of a Radical Christian.* Trans. Barbara and Martin Rumscheidt from *Gegenwind: Erinnerungen,* 1995. Minneapolis: Fortress Press, 1999.

Soelle, Dorothee. *The Silent Cry: Mysticism and Resistance.* Trans. Barbara and Martin Rumscheidt from *Mystik und Widerstand: "Du stilles Geschrei,"* 1997. Minneapolis: Fortress Press, 2001.

OTHER WORKS CITED

Soelle, Dorothee. "Between Matter and Spirit: Why and in What Sense Must Theology Be Materialist?" In *God of the Lowly: Socio-Historical Interpretations of the Bible,* ed. Willy Schottroff and Wolfgang Stegemann. Trans. Matthew J. O'Connell, 86–102. Maryknoll, NY: Orbis Books, 1984.

Soelle, Dorothee. "Christologie auf der Anklagebank." *Junge Kirche* 3 (1996): 130–40.

Soelle, Dorothee. "Mysticism, Liberation, and the Names of God." *Christianity and Crisis* 41, no. 11 (June 22, 1981): 179–85.

Soelle, Dorothee. "Remembering Christ: Faith, Theology, and Liberation." *Christianity and Crisis* 36, no. 10 (June 7, 1976): 136–41.

Soelle, Dorothee. "Resistance: Toward a First World Theology." *Christianity and Crisis* 39, no. 12 (July 23, 1979): 178–82.

Introduction

Around the world, many people have read the theological or political writings of Dorothee Soelle (1929–2003), or have heard her speak in such diverse locations as a church in Bremen, a peace rally in Washington, a classroom in El Salvador, or at the World Council of Churches. She has had a significant influence as a political activist, as a woman of deep wisdom and insightful spirituality, and as a theologian involved in a variety of "movements," from German political theology to anti-theodicy approaches to suffering to liberation theology with its political understandings of mysticism. She spoke and taught frequently in Germany, both in academic and church settings as well as at political rallies and protests. Soelle was a popular theologian and a professor at Union Theological Seminary in New York for over a decade (1975–87) but is probably just as well known for her involvement in anti-war protests and the peace movement and her connection to liberation movements in Latin America. Ultimately all of these activities were intimately intertwined for Soelle. Her influence is widespread, and most of her works are available on corner bookstore shelves in Germany and remain widely read in English; several have been translated into French and Spanish. She was a much-admired theologian and activist of the twentieth century whose prophetic voice and passionate vision of God still echo in the minds and hearts of many.

Soelle's vision of what living out the gospel means, of what true Christian spirituality is all about, offers a different conception of the spiritual life than we hear on many fronts today. Not one to be as concerned about organized religion as about living out God in the world, Soelle's brand of radical Christianity finds connections between mystical experience and political activism, between suffering and resisting the status quo. At a moment in American history when those who insist on the importance of religion's influence in politics lobby for monuments of the Ten Commandments in our courthouses and push for creationism to be taught in our schools, Dorothee Soelle's voice reminds us that God does not need our monuments or our public prayers of intercession as much as God needs our hands to bring about God's reign of justice in the world. She insisted that being Christian meant that one needed to stand against the war in Vietnam and was adamant that any theology that allowed soldiers to work in the gas chambers of Auschwitz and still go to church on Sunday must have some serious problems. Soelle called for a democratization of mysticism because experience of God is available for all and cannot be holed up in cathedrals or church dogmas. Like many others whose lives of the spirit are inspirational, Soelle seemed to have encountered and lived out God in ways that questioned much of what we accept as "given" about our world. Her critiques of capitalism, consumerism, nuclear arms buildup, Vietnam, and Christian theology that created the space for Auschwitz were all scathing.

Living in a society where success is the highest virtue and wealth its servant, what responsibility do we as human beings have for the tragedy of suffering and for the injustice of the world in which we live? Where is God in the midst of horrific human action such as that experienced at Auschwitz or in the lopsided distribution of resources and power that characterize our "global village"? Is there a vision of hope and redemption that takes those of us in the first world beyond the complacent, consumeristic cocoon in which we live and compels us to resist the very structures that bring us such so-called comfort? Is the traditional vision of God, separate from the world and intervening when it conforms to God's will or when people have enough faith, an accurate picture of the types of religious experiences people have today, of *real* spirituality? These are the types of questions that frame Soelle's work and drive her to insist that what she does is not to find a *logos*, a response focused on reason and scientific knowledge, but one that is rooted in myth and narrative, in poetry and prayer, in experience and history. Soelle's vision of the spiritual journey does not seek dogmatic answers to these concerns, but insists on the integrity of seeking to live our responses to them.

In 1965, Dorothee Soelle wrote her first theological book, *Stellvertretung: Ein Kapitel Theologie nach dem "Tode Gottes"* (English translation, 1967: *Christ the Representative: An Essay in Theology after the "Death of God"*). This book was not written as a dissertation to obtain her Ph.D. degree or as a book to further her career. Because she had no position as a professor in the German academic system, it did not shore up her reputation as a scholar. Soelle claims she wrote this text to figure out what she really believed, what she could hang on to and what she must discard, how she could talk of God after the horrors of Auschwitz, how she could be a German Christian with her sense of shame in the latter half of the twentieth century, how she could "find clarity" in the face of her situation.[1] This sense of her motivation in writing a book on Christology is characteristic of all Soelle's work: it is an expression of her deep faith and action trying to find voice and insight to further her praxis and continue changing the world. In order to understand the insights of Soelle's spirituality, then, we must begin with the context of her life and her experiences.

Soelle's journey is rooted in her experience as a German teen-ager in the aftermath of Auschwitz and Hiroshima. In response to these horrors, a God whose omnipotence and control were emphasized seemed an impossibility for her. The overwhelm-ing suffering and evil of the Holocaust clearly indicted belief in a benevolent God up above in the starry sky controlling the events in the world. The idea of chalking the horrors up to a "bigger plan" made God a sadist in Soelle's estimation. God as transcendent and powerful, separate from the world and con-trolling it, could no longer be taken seriously; yet it was this view of God Soelle found in the German Protestantism that ex-isted in her youth. At the same time, Soelle's liberal bourgeois upbringing, which was more philosophically than religiously minded, offered her no comfort in the aftermath of Auschwitz, either. People she knew who were good, educated, liberal Ger-mans had done nothing to stop Hitler. Optimism and hope in light of these events seemed impossible. Soelle's continuing search for a way to live and believe after the Holocaust is the backdrop to her vision of the spiritual life, to her idea of the experience of God in the world.

The much heralded "death of God" proclaimed by radical Christian theologians in the 1960s was to some degree one response to the horrific tragedies and massive suffering which characterized the first half of the twentieth century. The super-natural God, separate from the world and able to control at least to some degree what happened in the world, was in seri-ous trouble for some important reasons: (1) modern society no longer "needed" God to explain the world because science was taking care of that task, making God not only superfluous, but even anti-scientific in the minds of many, and (2) radical suf-fering, evidenced especially in the abhorrent acts of inhumanity during two World Wars and the Holocaust, indicted whoever or whatever was "in charge" of the world for allowing such unimaginable horrors to occur. For many, the transcendence of God was relinquished in favor of immanence — what we do here and now in history is all that matters; there is nothing more, nothing less; it is immanence all the way down. If there was any acknowledgment of the possibility of God's transcendence, it somehow remained separate from the thrust of people's lives in the world. With so many books on spirituality that largely focus on ways to *separate* ourselves from the muck of the world, transcendence is still often kept separate from what one does on a day-to-day basis. Soelle describes the epitome of this separation of our world into spheres which do not intersect or even touch one another by using the example of German soldiers who put people to death in gas chambers while wearing belts with buckles which proclaimed "God with us," and then went home to listen to Bach. One's spirituality is seen as something that happens individually, separate from most of the normal, everyday "stuff" that goes on in our lives.

In response to this world where God seems either superfluous or somehow separate from the world, Dorothee Soelle offers a compelling vision of how our experiences of God are actually part of the world in which we live. Soelle acknowledges that in a scientific world we cannot take "the supreme being once called 'God' " for granted, but she remains hesitant, after Martin Buber, to claim a *logos* about God, insisting instead that God must remain a "You," a "Thou," one we address, and "not in some sense an *object* of our 'knowledge,' an 'It.' "[2] For Soelle, the question "does God exist?" is not the most important one because God is not a being alongside the world. She suggests instead that we recognize God in the experiences of transformation, the moments of salvation that take place *in the world*. It is in such experiences that we know God as God. We do not experience God in ways that lift us out of the world, but in ways that connect us even more deeply to the world. Thus it is a certain form of mysticism, with a focus on finding God in everyday experiences and recognizing the connectedness and union of all creation, that permeates Soelle's work.

One of the mystics whose work most keenly influenced Soelle is Meister Eckhart, the medieval theologian whose mystical vision subverted the clear ordering of the universe that constituted the medieval worldview: a hierarchy with God at the top, angels underneath, men then women, animals then plants, each with decreasing status and value. Everyone and everything had its appropriate place and its appropriate tasks. Medieval mysticism's suggestion that our goal was union with God called into question that neat and tidy ordering of authority and value. How could one even imagine union with God in such a hierarchically ordered world? God had "his" place in the structure and we as human beings had ours, and never the twain shall meet — much less become one.

Similarly, Dorothee Soelle's mystical-political theology for the contemporary world offers a clear subversion of the worldview for our time. Her identification of transcendence as "radical immanence . . . immanence loved and affirmed at the roots"[3] suggests a re-visioning of religious experience that moves from a supernatural, separate-from-the-world encounter with God to an understanding that God is completely, "radically" embedded in and related to creation at its very core. Experiences of a God whose transcendence is radically embedded in creation are not mediated by institutions demanding order and obedience; such experiences of God are mediated in history, in creation, in other people. In other words, experiences of God emerge out of our relationships to *all* that is "other," not a relationship to a specific other being. This mystical understanding of relationship with God subverts structures and authorities that exist, it subverts traditional conceptions of power as power over, and it subverts autonomy and independence as ideals.

A God whose transcendence is radically immanent provides a way to subvert power and authority embodied in structures and institutions as well as in social and cultural values and ideologies. For Soelle, this means that our mystical spirituality is always political at its core. God is more than creation, but is not separate from creation. God can be mediated only through the world—through other people, nature, sociopolitical structures, and sometimes even religious institutions. Thus our spirituality, our living out God in the world, does not separate us from the world, but acknowledges instead that God is "bound into the web of life"[4] and thus our relationship with God makes us equally part of that web. We are called to be participants in life, resisting the status quo in whatever ways it harms any part of that interdependent web as we seek to make God's justice real in the world.

Soelle's attempts to speak of this God necessarily push her away from the dogmatic language of her tradition, whose reason is too narrow to express encounters with the transcendent/immanent God of most people's experiences. Soelle insisted that one must begin from experience and history, and not from the doctrines handed down. Thus Soelle's spiritual vision is filled with poetry, with prayer, with stories, with conversations — with life.

•

Dorothee Soelle was born in Cologne, Germany, in 1929, and grew up during the years of Hitler, the Nazi regime, and World War II. Her parents were German liberals, well-educated and ensuring their children were the same. Her parents opposed the Nazis, even hiding a Jewish woman in their house for a time to protect her. As a child, Soelle explains, she was really apolitical and wished mainly that the hours spent in air-raid shelters and the preoccupation of the adults in her life with such matters as simply finding enough food would stop.[5] At the end of the war, dealing with the fallenness of Germany and her sense of loss of national identity became the focus of Soelle's adolescence. She identifies this time as the "fog of my German, romantic, bourgeois-educated youth."[6]

It was only in Soelle's later attempts to make sense of life in Germany after World War II that the political implications of her heritage came to a head. She felt the shame of a generation asking itself how the horrors of Auschwitz could happen, struggling with what they or their parents did or did not do to stop the Nazis. Soelle realized that "the liberal bourgeois culture had ended in Auschwitz; some of the elite leaders had been as cultivated as my parents."[7] The optimism of that liberalism died in the recognition that this liberal bourgeois culture had done nothing to stop the war or the control of fascists. Out of these struggles, it is Soelle's wrestling with a "deep sense of shame" that defines her lifelong journey of dealing with her history. As she describes it,

> I need this shame about my people; I do not want to forget anything, because forgetting nurtures the illusion that it is possible to be a truly human being without the lessons of the dead. The truth of the matter is that we need their help.[8]

Soelle writes that she grew up on Goethe rather than the Bible, in good German, liberal, bourgeois tradition. With a heritage formed more from the Enlightenment than Luther, Soelle had a somewhat perfunctory relationship to Christianity. After the war, when she recognized that this Protestant liberalism had been helpless to stand against the atrocities, Soelle searched for a "new" home and found it in the church fringes. As she describes it, "I did not intend to 'come home' to church, since I mistrusted this institution deeply. I went home to Pascal and Kierkegaard, to the early Luther — all of them being homeless in the established churches."[9] This embracing of a nonestablishment Christianity that was unable to find a home in religious institutions would continue to mark her theological vision and her relationship with the church over the years. It also goes hand in hand with her opposition to authoritarianism in its many forms as key to the Christian life.

Soelle claims that liberalism's failure to stand for anything in protest goes together with its failure to accord every human being the dignity insisted upon in Christianity. While she was more than willing to let go of the intellectually indefensible aspects of Christian heritage like the virgin birth or literal miracles, Soelle notes that Jesus always continued to have a hold on her. His powerless love was ultimately more compelling than the omnipotent, controlling "Father" God of her youth. It is this hold that kept her struggling with some form of Christianity as a possible haven, even in the face of ecclesiastical packaging of Jesus that was not acceptable to her.[10]

It was Rudolf Bultmann's project of demythologization that provided the liberation from an intellectually questionable Christianity for Soelle. Bultmann's willingness to recognize the mythical character of the stories in the Bible and his attempt to reinterpret those myths for a scientific age allowed Soelle the intellectual to engage Christianity more seriously. As she explains Bultmann's appeal, "One cannot live with one foot in the age of science and the other in the world of myth. Such a contradiction empties reason of responsibility and makes faith an escape from reality."[11] Acknowledging the responsibility that is concomitant with reason and faith was of key importance to Soelle, plagued as she was by the memories of Auschwitz and what she saw as a lack of responsibility taken by many during World War II. If the mythic thinking of the Bible could be distorted to affirm

If science (biology) had been used to justify Nazi eugenics, does that make "it" unacceptable?

obedience to the authority of Hitler, then such an interpretation of Christianity was unacceptable. The push for responsibility that goes beyond one's individual beliefs, actions, and conversions is what separated Soelle from Bultmann and compelled her political activity and her turn to a political spirituality.

Through Soelle's first marriage to painter Dietrich Soelle in 1954 and her later marriage to Fulbert Steffensky in 1969, she had four children. When she writes of certain moments of insight as she tells the story of her life and her theology, these events often occur in connection with her children. Whether it was Caroline's observation when entering an "awful" church that there was, "No God in there"[12] or Soelle's realization that it was okay to feed her children fish sticks instead of gourmet food so she could pursue her work, her experiences as a mother seemed to further shape and confirm her vision of a different picture of God. The experience of being a single parent after her separation and divorce from her first husband clarified her sense of the importance of both work and partnership with others. Soelle experienced the strong pulls of her sense of vocation and the importance of doing good work, at the same time that others criticized the "sacrifices" her children made because of the work their mother did and because she was divorced. The importance of her children and her connection especially to her second partner, Fulbert Steffensky, at times left her at odds with some feminists she encountered. Soelle claims that while she wanted a different world, a world free from the confines of patriarchy, the focus for her was not on rejecting motherhood or marriage, but in focusing on the kind of world where persons could learn "to work and to love," as her famous book on the theology of creation put it. The experience of the pain of giving birth connected her to a vision of the pain of God, the God who suffers with us, who is affected by the process of birth in the world. Having children and a partner was absolutely affirmed for her theologically in the vision of mutuality and interdependence that characterize her vision of God and the world.

Soelle's involvement in the peace movement, and specifically her work with the Politische Nachtgebet (Political Evensong) in Cologne beginning in the late 1960s, brought to the fore the second situation that would have a politicizing effect on her life and work. As this ecumenical group of Catholics, Protestants, and others met together to discuss theological questions and their political implications in the late 1960s, war in Vietnam was underway and provided the focus for many of their reflections and actions. As Soelle describes the group's efforts, "Our pattern was to provide political information integrated with biblical texts, a brief address, calls for action, and finally, discussion with the gathered congregation. The basic elements of all subsequent Evensongs were information, meditations, and action."[13] There were many socialist elements in the work of the group as they pushed for political action emerging from their theological work together. There were attempts at repression of the group, and some who collaborated with the Political Evensong ran into employment problems.

Soelle's "conversion" from liberalism to "radical-democratic socialism" emerged from this Political Evensong and its engagement with the Vietnam War. She claims that this war "unmasked capitalism more than any other historical fact during her lifetime."[14] She visited Vietnam in the early 1970s and found out firsthand the real nature of Western imperialism which existed in relationship to Vietnam. These insights pushed her involvement in Christian-Marxist dialogue even further and encouraged her embrace of Marxism as an important analytical tool. Concepts of alienation and class struggle became part and parcel of Soelle's work, helping her to recognize "the deep this-worldliness of Christian faith,"[15] and the importance of "the historical and social dimension of human existence."[16] When some of the official dialogues between Christians and Marxists in the first world broke down in the late 1960s, the conversations found new homes in third world contexts. Soelle views Marxism not as providing an all-encompassing ideology which overshadows Christianity, but instead as offering important analytical tools for understanding the historical and social world. According to Soelle, the use of Marxist theory by Christians involved in a theology of liberation "re-instrumentalized theology instead of ideologizing it."[17]

While already a popular author and a well-known public figure because of her involvement in the Politische Nachtgebet, Soelle struggled to establish herself in the German academic world. When initially attempting to defend her *Habilitation* in 1971 at the University of Cologne, she failed, the first person to do so since 1945.[18] Her failure was partially connected with political conflicts between the liberals and conservatives. Soelle's association with Marxism and various political movements was only one of the reasons for this situation, though. Soelle explains that her work was seen as "not academic enough, not pious enough and not politically mainstream enough" for an academic career in Germany.[19] Soelle describes the impetus for her work when she states, "I wanted to document my thought process, not my knowledge."[20] She later also recognized that sexism played a part in her academic rejection. She quotes a newspaper headline from the *Frankfurter Rundschau* concerning a conflict she had with the theology faculty at the University of Mainz to explain: "Leftist and a woman — that's going too far."[21] While she later successfully passed her *Habilitation*, it is not surprising that the United States turned out to be more of an academic "home" for Soelle in many ways.

Soelle was invited to be a visiting professor at Union Theological Seminary in New York City in 1975. While this was a complicated endeavor because of negotiating the position of her husband, Fulbert Steffensky, she and Steffensky came to the United States and Soelle ended up teaching as a visiting professor at Union from 1975 to 1987. Soelle found at Union a more welcome place for her combination of political and theological work and her form of radical Christianity. The countercultural movements, such as the women's movement, the civil rights movement, and the peace movement, which were very much alive in the 1970s, had a more prominent place in the academic world of the United States than in Germany. While Soelle had often felt the need to apologize for being Christian among the socialists in Germany, she found Christianity and socialism in much closer relationship among many members of these counterculture groups in the United States.

Soelle also credits her time at Union Seminary with awakening her feminism. Much of Soelle's early work is not explicitly feminist, though with hindsight one can see glimpses of feminist themes throughout even her initial writings.[22] These themes became much more explicit as Soelle's students and colleagues continued to ask her what her theology had to do with her being a woman. Her willingness to connect the personal and the political, her demand that we continue to ask how our theology is affected by and is different because of the event of the Holocaust, and her unwillingness to play the academic game of finding more and more authorities to shore up one's own theological stance were all ways she had begun her feminist work, and which she finally acknowledged explicitly with the help of her Union friends.[23] Feminist themes became core to Soelle's theology in the 1980s and beyond.

It is clear that Auschwitz and Vietnam were the origins of Soelle's politicization, and her political shifts connected her to the German political theology movement associated with Johannes Baptist Metz and Jürgen Moltmann.[24] Political theology

is seen as a response to secularization, characterized as "the hu-
manization of the world, the absence of a starting point in man
or nature for our knowledge of God, and the destruction of
direct religious certainty in the wake of Western European enlightenment."[25] Metz, Moltmann, and Soelle all use the "death
of God" in some sense to describe this modern situation —
that is, the death of the omnipotent, controlling God "out
there" — and contend that the existentialism of the early twentieth century does not help the crisis. Soelle's initial engagement
with the political horizon of theology is clearly part of this
German political theology movement and instrumental in her
radicalization.

Yet it is a theology of liberation that ultimately came to be
Soelle's self-declared home. The emphasis on praxis, reflection,
and renewed praxis as theological method in liberation theology offered Soelle helpful categories for articulating her vision
of the relationship between theology and the realm of the political. The strong use of Marxist analysis in Latin American
liberation theology also provided clear connections to her work
with Marxism. Soelle's visits to Latin America, especially Nicaragua and Argentina, prompted several books and articles that
were reflections on the situation of the people there and the
theological insights gained from the injustice they faced and
the theological wisdom they offered.[26] She was deeply affected
by the poetry of Ernesto Cardenal, the disappearance of Ernst
Käsemann's daughter in Argentina, and the reality of the oppression and murder of the poor as they struggled for liberation.
According to Soelle, it is imperative that we in the first world
listen to the voices of the poor from developing countries in
order to criticize our own priorities.[27] It is only as people in the
first world hear the voices of the marginalized that we recognize
values in our society that foster injustice, recognition that often
does not occur if we only hear the television advertisements or

read the scriptures in the way they have always been read to support the *status quo.*

This struggle for liberation in a first world context also compelled Soelle's continued involvement in the peace movement, especially in opposition to the nuclear arms buildup in Germany and the United States. She was involved with other radical Christians in both countries in acts of civil disobedience against the arms race.[28] She rejected the rhetoric of "security" that fueled the arms race and pushed instead for our opening of a "window of vulnerability." Her active work as part of the peace movement continued throughout her life as a cornerstone for her vision of the Christian life and her understanding of God.

Soelle continued to live out her vision of the Christian life by her work as a political activist and through the narrative and prayer that characterized her theological writings. She died in the spring of 2003 of a heart attack while leading a workshop with her husband. Those lauding her life and work were numerous, and amazingly included people across the theological and political spectrums. The bishop of Nordelbein, the Right Reverend Bärbel von Wartenberg-Potter, who offered her funeral sermon, said, "Her words are like bread — texts full of clarity and concrete life experience, honest, nourishing, and illuminating."[29] Soelle remains very much alive in the words and memories, thoughts and feelings, protests and love of those of us affected by her life, her work, her passion, her spirit. She wrote, "I am irreplaceable only for those who love me,"[30] and so she is.

•

As I write this, I can look up to see a picture of me standing with Dorothee Soelle in her study in Hamburg, almost as if she is watching over my attempts to gather her writings and introduce something of her vision. Dorothee and I are both laughing in the picture, at what I can't remember right now. I had the opportunity to spend time with Dorothee in Chicago and then later in Hamburg in 1997, while I was working on my dissertation on her work. I was honored by the opportunity to have extended informal conversations as well as formal interviews with her, riding in a car in Chicago, interviewing her during a train ride to Bremen, sharing a simple supper with her and Fulbert before interviewing her in her study in Hamburg. Unlike some theologians and spiritual writers whose works I have read who seemed somehow totally different than I expected when I met them, Soelle was exactly how I imagined. The theology she wrote emerged from the life she lived, convinced as she was that what each of us does in the world really matters and that the "city of god" might just be possible. After studying her writings and her life, after encountering God in her works, I share her hope.

Dorothee Soelle's theological writings span almost forty years and cover a range of theological topics. Her corpus includes books of poetry, monographs, collections of essays, and dozens of articles on topics ranging from socialism to prayer. Soelle's work is seldom doctrinally based and has been described as unsystematic.[31] Even her *Thinking about God,* while covering the basic topics of a systematic theology, reads more like a collection of essays than a sustained systematic work. Her unsystematic approach has at times led to Soelle's contributions being overlooked since her perspective on a given topic is usually distributed throughout her works. Soelle's style is not unlike that of Martin Luther, who also wrote mainly in response to issues and situations that arose rather than always attempting to provide systematic coverage. While some may interpret such a description of her work as a criticism, I see her approach providing an immediacy to her theology and her view of the spiritual life that is often missing in theological writings.

I interviewed Soelle in 1997, and it is telling that when I asked her what she considered her most significant works, she named her books of poetry along with her magnum opus, *Mystik und Widerstand: "Du stilles Geschrei"* (English: *The Silent Cry: Mysticism and Resistance*).[32] These choices are indicative of the uniqueness of her theological vision, as well as the enduring importance she places on both the language of poetry, and the mystical approach to God in her work.

Soelle's writings are extensive, though many of them are frequently overlooked. Some of her most popular works in English are still in print, but, alas, many are not. Yet some of her most insightful moments occur in texts that are not readily available. The selections for this book coalesce around three "different" motifs that provide key lenses for looking at Soelle's work: a different understanding of religious experience focused on mysticism and a revisioning of God's power and thus the nature of our relationship to God; a different view of the spiritual journey that has at its heart an engagement with the suffering of the world and our resistance to the causes of that suffering in our politics and in our everyday decisions; and a different view of the language used to express these experiences and journeys, focused less on a theological *logos* and more on narrative, poetry, and prayer.

I have included selections from some of her well-known writings, but also have incorporated some hidden gems that are less widely read. The selections range from poetry to personal memoir to theological treatise, but all of them include stories of Soelle's experiences of life, for these are at the core of her vision of God. It is difficult to segregate Soelle's writings into specific subject categories, because the main themes of her work tend to show up in almost all her writings. Thus while each section provides a common theme around which all of the selections revolve, the categories are not neatly divided and a number of the pieces could have been included in all three categories.

As with the collection of any texts that include writings from periods prior to our contemporary attention to gender issues in our use of language, this collection of Soelle's works contains early writings with exclusive language for humanity. I have left these original translations in place because they reflect an earlier time in Soelle's theology before she was explicitly conscious of certain aspects of gender issues herself. I have also chosen not to change earlier male references for God, because Soelle begins her expansion of images and language for God fairly early in her writings as she turns to mystical ideas, and the shifts in language correspond in some ways with aspects of her own theological development.

In the end, I hope that this text provides at least a glimpse of the vision of the spiritual life that Soelle wrote about and lived, for it is a compelling one that continues to affect me some sixteen years after I began studying her work. I read Soelle initially in my first semester of seminary, when my insightful theology professor had us read her *To Work and to Love: A Theology of Creation*. Because Soelle's vision pushed me to ask new questions about God's purpose for human beings and how that related to our economic systems, my relationship to capitalism was forever changed. Soelle's work is like that. You cannot read her stories, her theology, or her poetry and remain unaffected. You cannot have met her and fail to ask a new set of questions. Her spiritual vision is grounded in a desire to push all of us to talk about our religious experiences, to question the vision of God that has often been handed on by our religious institutions, to insist that any system that fails to live up to God's vision of justice must be opposed actively and insistently, to recognize real love in a powerless man from Nazareth who loved all the way to the end and beyond. May we all catch something of Soelle's vision.

NOTES

1. Dorothee Soelle, *Against the Wind: Memoir of a Radical Christian*, trans. Barbara and Martin Rumscheidt (Minneapolis: Fortress Press, 1999), 32.

2. Dorothee Soelle, *Thinking about God: An Introduction to Theology*, trans. John Bowden (Philadelphia: Trinity Press International, 1990), 171, emphasis mine.

3. Ibid., 190, 192.

4. Ibid., 189.

5. *Against the Wind*, 3.

6. Ibid., 17.

7. Dorothee Soelle, *Beyond Mere Dialogue: On Being Christian and Socialist* (Detroit: CFS, 1982), 1.

8. *Against the Wind*, 17.

9. *Beyond Mere Dialogue*, 2.

10. *Against the Wind*, 28.

11. Ibid., 29.

12. Ibid., 167.

13. *Against the Wind*, 38.

14. *Beyond Mere Dialogue*, 2.

15. Ibid., 18.

16. *Against the Wind*, 50.

17. Ibid., 52.

18. Dorothee Soelle, interview by author, tape recording and transcript, Hamburg, Germany, July 20, 1997.

19. Ibid.

20. *Against the Wind*, 67.

21. Ibid., 66.

22. These certainly include her anti-authoritarian stance, her recognition of the importance of the body and material existence in doing theology, and her dethroning of the otherworldly, omnipotent "God as King" understanding of God.

23. *Against the Wind*, 66.

24. See especially Johannes Baptist Metz, *Theology of the World* (New York: Herder, 1969), and Jürgen Moltmann, *Theology of Hope: On the Ground and the Implications of a Christian Eschatology*, trans. James W. Leitch (New York: Harper & Row, 1967).

25. Frances P. Fiorenza, "Political Theology and Liberation Theology: An Inquiry into Their Fundamental Meaning," in *Liberation, Revolution, and Freedom: Theological Perspectives*, ed. Thomas M. McFadden,

Proceedings of the College Theology Society (New York: Seabury Press, 1975), 6.

26. These include *Stations of the Cross: A Latin American Pilgrimage,* trans. Joyce Irwin from *Gott im Müll: Eine andere Entdeckung Latinamerikas,* 1992 (Minneapolis: Fortress Press, 1993), and *On Earth as in Heaven: A Liberation Spirituality of Sharing,* trans. Marc Batko (Louisville: Westminster/John Knox Press, 1993), *Of War and Love,* trans. Rita and Robert Kimber from *Im Hause des Menschenfressers: Texte zum Frieden,* 1981 (Maryknoll, NY: Orbis Books, 1983), as well as numerous essays.

27. *Against the Wind,* 104.

28. Dorothee Soelle, *The Window of Vulnerability: A Political Spirituality,* trans. Linda M. Maloney from *Das Fenster der Verwundbarkeit: Theologisch-politische Texte,* 1990 (Minneapolis: Fortress Press, 1990), 144.

29. Bärbel von Wartenberg-Potter, "Funeral Sermon," in *The Theology of Dorothee Soelle,* ed. Sarah K. Pinnock (Harrisburg, PA: Trinity Press International, 2003), viii.

30. Dorothee Soelle, *Christ the Representative: An Essay in Theology after the "Death of God,"* trans. David Lewis from *Stellvertretung: Ein Kapitel Theologie nach dem "Tode Gottes,"* 1965 (London: SCM Press, 1967), 46.

31. For example, see Mary Hembrow Snyder, "The Ideas of God and Suffering in the Political Theology of Dorothee Sölle," in *Pluralism and Oppression: Theology in World Perspective,* ed. Paul F. Knitter, Annual Publication of the College Theological Society, 1988, vol. 34 (Lanham, MD: University Press of America, 1991), 250.

32. Dorothee Sölle, interview by author, tape recording and transcript, Hamburg, Germany, July 21, 1997. Her two books of poetry in English are *Revolutionary Patience,* trans. Robert and Rita Kimber from *Die revolutionäre Geduld,* 1974 (Maryknoll, NY: Orbis Books, 1974); and *Of War and Love,* trans. Rita and Robert Kimber from *Im Hause des Menschenfressers: Texte zum Frieden,* 1981 (Maryknoll, NY: Orbis Books, 1983). She also published varying collections of poetry in German, some overlapping with these English versions. When I interviewed her she had just finished *Mystik und Widerstand: "Du stilles Geschrei"* (Hamburg: Hoffmann und Kampe, 1997), since translated into English as *The Silent Cry: Mysticism and Resistance,* trans. Barbara and Martin Rumscheidt (Minneapolis: Fortress Press, 2001).

1

A Different Experience
Power and Mysticism

In this first section, the writings included largely focus on
Soelle's mystical vision of the nature of religious experience and
her view of God as one who is vulnerable because the power
of God is powerless love. "Different experience" encompasses
Soelle's understanding that religious experience does not look to
obedience to dogmas or church teachings as its core, nor does it
search for moments that separate us from the everyday world.
She rejects the focus on a supernatural God who is separate
from the world and seeks to pull us out of the world and instead turns to a mystical vision of a God who encompasses the
whole world and into whom we sink as the very ground of our
existence in the world. For Soelle, such a vision of God pushes
us to recognize God in the world, embracing all that is and
present in everything. This also means that we no longer speak
of God "out there," but as that which is integral and connected
to every single aspect of our life in the world. Nothing is secular
for Soelle, for the God who is radically incarnated in our midst
sacralizes everything. Mysticism is not something for the chosen
few, but that which needs to be democratized so that all can see

[handwritten margin note: Vision of Religious Experience & God.]

that of God which surrounds them and all can have the opportunity to express such experiences. God is involved in our lives, our loves, our work, and our politics. This involvement is not in the form of commands from on high that provide rules for us to obey, nor in the control of every event so that everything is willed by God, nor in the insistence on using the word "God" in public places, but in the form of the very interdependent web of life through which all of creation is connected. Power is re-visioned as empowerment, so that good power is always shared between God and creation rather than used by an omnipotent God as a mechanism of control. Thus religious experience is about our connectedness to the very ground of our existence, our relationship with God who is bound into the web of life.

EXPERIENCE, NOT AUTHORITY

The best definition of mysticism, the classical definition, is a *cognitio Dei experimentalis,* a perception of God through experience. This means an awareness of God gained not through books, not through the authority of religious teachings, not through the so-called priestly office but through the life experiences of human beings, experiences that are articulated and reflected upon in religious language but that first come to people in what they encounter in life, independent of the church's institutions.

Mysticism can occur, then, in all religions; and it almost always clashes head-on with the hierarchy dominant in its time. It is an experience of God, an experience of being one with God, an experience that God bestows on people. It is a call that people hear or perceive, an experience that breaks through the existing limitations of human comprehension, feeling, and reflection. This element of shattering old limitations is crucial to the mystical experience, and it is responsible for the difficulty of communicating mystical experience: It is impossible to speak about what lies beyond the capabilities of speech, yet anyone who has had mystical experience feels compelled to speak about it. The language he or she uses will therefore be paradoxical, self-contradictory, and obscure. Or it may lead to silence, for silence is one of the modes of mystical experience.

What I would like to stress here is that we should not regard mystics as people at some great remove from ourselves, nor as people with unique experiences incomprehensible to all the rest of us. One of the greatest mystics and probably the greatest German mystic, Meister Eckhart, never — as far as we are able to tell — saw visions or heard voices. He reflected on religious experience without reference to these specific visionary or auditory phenomena. The crucial point here is that in the mystical understanding of God, experience is more important than doctrine, the inner light more important than church authority, the certainty of God and communication with him more important than believing in his existence or positing his existence rationally.

Here, too, I would like to give an example, one that did not originally come under the heading of mysticism but that illustrates the broad sense in which I understand this concept. During a class at the seminary where I teach in New York, the question of religious experiences came up. An embarrassed silence followed, of course. No one in this generation will admit to such experiences or can talk about them. Finally, though, a young woman raised her hand, and a week later she reported on her religious experience. What she had to say made a profound impression on me.

She told how she used to read a great deal when she was fourteen, especially at night, like so many of us. Her parents did not allow her to stay up late, because she was supposed to be asleep and living a well-ordered life. One night she had read in bed for several hours and then, waking suddenly at four in the morning with her head full of what she had been reading, she went out into the winter night, looked at the stars, and had — as she told it — a feeling of happiness that was unique for her, a feeling of unity with all of life, with God, an experience of overpowering clarity and joy, a sense of being cared for and borne up: No ill can befall me; I am indestructible; I am one with the All. This was the kind of language she used to describe her experience. She then went on to say that she didn't have this experience again until later in her life and in a totally different context. This other context was a major demonstration against the Vietnam War. There, too, she felt cared for, a part of the All, felt herself together with others participating in the truth of the All. For her, both these experiences belonged together under the heading "religious experience."

If this same young woman had lived in fourteenth-century Germany, she probably would have said, "I heard a voice, and it said to me, 'I am with you' " — or something like that. Or she might have said, "I saw a light." In the twentieth century, she can't use that kind of language to communicate her experiences to others. She has to struggle with the language and with her own embarrassment. We have no language at all that can describe these experiences precisely, yet she had the courage to try to tell us what she had felt. And I would guess that if you look back on your own life history, you will recall similar experiences, states of "being high," to use the banal expression, states related to mental and spiritual experiences for which religious language provides a kind of home or mode of expression.

Mystical experience is not, then, something extraordinary, requiring some special talent or sixth sense. Thousands of people in other cultures have had such experiences, experiences of this happiness, this wholeness, this sense of being at home in the

world, of being at one with God. It makes no difference — and
this point has been confirmed by everyone who has ever reported on mystical experience — whether these experiences are
interpreted with the aid of a personal God or nontheistically,
as in oriental mysticism. Whether we see these experiences in
terms of the Tao or of God is not central to them. How we
view them will depend on the culture we live in, our past experiences, the languages we have learned. What is appalling in
our culture is that most people have no language at all for de-
scribing such experiences. And the result of that is, of course,
that these experiences go uncommunicated to others, are lost
and forgotten. We are unable to tell anyone else about the most
important experiences we have.   —SW, 86–89

NO HIGHER POWER

There is no room in mystical devotion for the recognition of a
higher power, the worship of lordship or the denial of our own
strength. On the contrary, the master-slave relationship is very
often expressly criticized in mystical texts. But above all it is
surpassed through creative language. Here religion is the feeling
of oneness with the whole, intimate connection, not subjugation; human beings do not honor God because of his power
and lordship, but submerge themselves in him, or, as they always say, in his love. He is the ground, as Meister Eckhart says,
love, depth, sea. Such nature symbols are preferred where God
demands no obedience but union, where a distant other does
not demand sacrifice and renunciation of self, where harmony
and oneness with the living become the theme of religion.
    In this religion the most important virtue is then no longer
obedience but solidarity. Out of the power-word "father" comes
the freeing and unifying one; out of the objects which we are

come subjects who are involved in this process. Rather than expecting something to come from above, we learn to think cooperatively. This all belongs to mystical devotion.

Emancipation does not mean only to get rid of the oppressive colonialist and to be freed *from* God who imprisons us. It also has to be positively stated: We have to talk about our freedom *for* a different God. Mystical language is an aid to express a deeper devotion than patriarchal language is able to. In traditional theology and churchy talk, we talk about God's relationship to humankind in verbs that imply human passivity, such as: direct, control, send, use, proclaim, judge, shape, confront, confirm, destroy, offer, and rule over humankind. When we reflect on the implications of this traditional language we will find it as inadequate and dangerous as the sexist exclusives "he" and "his" in reference to humankind. Our need for a better, nonhierarchical language will then grow, and we may use verbs for God's activity that leave enough space for human response, such as: evoke, empower, liberate, support, build, awaken, listen, nourish, summon, suffer, experience, participate, rejoice, and stand within. Mystical language is full of God symbols and expressions of God's action which are free of domination.   — "Mysticism," 183–84

GOD HAPPENS

[In Martin Buber's idea that "In the beginning was the relationship,"] God is not spoken of as the supreme object, but as the mutual, significant, actively experienced relationship to life. God is not found as a precious stone or as blue flowers, as Novalis pictured, but God happens. God spent this Tuesday afternoon with me — that is a meaningful statement, an attempt to identify the experience, the encounter, which puts us in relationship. The search is then subsequently often understood as a wrong road. Our everyday life, our real, inconspicuous relationships, were all too hazy to us. What takes place in the encounter with God is that the searching ends not with finding, but with being found. God was always already standing behind me, even when I was rushing in the other direction.

A theological consequence of this approach by the God who encounters us is the linguistic form in which we can communicate God. Only secondarily can it be the principle, the awareness, the dogma. Religious language destroys itself if it talks about God in the I-It relationship. Prayer or narrative is possible talk of God. In the narratives of the New Testament God appears, God happens. If we tell stories of God and are concerned about the narrative method, we are telling what God does or how God conceals himself, how God acts. And in prayer we ask God to do something worth telling of, to appear, to show power for good, to change us. In these two linguistic forms we talk of God more as an event than as a substance. We speak from and to God, instead of "about" him.

The question which is often put to me, "Do you believe in God?," usually seems a superficial one. If it only means that there is an extra place in your head where God sits, then God is in no way an event which changes your whole life, an event from which, as Buber says of real revelation, I do not emerge unchanged. We should really ask, "Do you live out God?" That would be in keeping with the reality of the experience.

Criticism of the false ontology of being-in-oneself and the theology of the God who is in himself is nowadays made from various directions. Biblical thought in its otherness, the personalism of Martin Buber, the basic Marxist idea of the priority of those who work and suffer over the needs of capital and its "material pressures," existentialist philosophy with its attempt to deobjectify people, process theology with its conception of the God who develops further, who cannot remain behind the ethical level of the democratic consciousness, but above all feminist theology with its insistence on a relational, nonpatriarchal language, which is in a position to communicate experiences with God existentially — these are attempts to overcome the ontological lack of relationship and to think of God beyond theism and atheism.

One of the most difficult problems in this connection is the question of the power of this God of relationship, this God of the life which calls and answers. Is not the God of the powerless also powerless, the God of women also pushed to the periphery and trivialized, the God of the peacemakers also unprotected and an object of mockery? So why do Christians refer to a higher being if this God is not omnipotent? What does it mean to think in theological terms of God's renunciation of power, which shapes the story of Jesus of Nazareth?

The Christian assumption that we recognize God most clearly in this figure of someone tortured to death goes completely against our fixation on power and domination. Christ appears in the Gospels as the man for others, has nothing but his love: no weapons, no magical tricks, no privileges. It is false christology to imagine Christ as a Greek god, a figure who can do anything, and who has a return ticket to heaven. That is really a denial of the incarnation. Christ refused to do miracles if they were asked of him as a proof. He refused to come down from the cross, and the original witnesses understood that quite clearly, when they mocked him and said, "If you are the Son of God, come down from the cross and then we will believe in you" (Matt. 27:42). For those who mocked him, God was identical with power and rule. But the only capital with which he came into the world was his love, and it was as powerless and as powerful as love is. He had nothing but his love with which to win our heart. Perhaps the abstractness of the search for the meaning of life can be overcome where we do not find the back-up of a father but the face of a human being at the center of power. In fact we are not saved by any "higher being, god, emperor or tribune," as the Internationale puts it. No higher being can save us, because the only salvation is to become love. More than that is not promised to us. All other deliverance is based on a mere shift from a bad state to a good state, to another place, to another time, which does not change us in the process. Such hope for power, for the intervention of an omnipotent superiority and unassailability, has always deceived people. God is not the extension of our false wishes, nor the projection of our imperialisms.

And yet that is still not the whole story. It is possible to understand the cross of Christ in this language of powerless love, but it is impossible to articulate the resurrection as long as we regard all power as "evil," as tyrannical, as split off and masculine. I note that tendency in a critical attitude to my own theology, which can be understood in three different stages. I had left behind belief in an omnipotent father "who rules all things so gloriously," derived from theism. For me, the metaphor of the "death of God" meant deliberately giving up the notion of the omnipotence of God as theologically and ethically impossible. In the light of Auschwitz the assumption of the omnipotence of God seemed — and still seems! — to me to be a heresy, a misunderstanding of what God means. From this criticism of the theistic-patriarchal God I developed a position in which the cross of Christ stands in the center, as an affirmation of the nonviolent impotence of love in which God himself is no longer one who imposes suffering, but a fellow sufferer.

The difficulty of this position is connected with the question of the power of this nonviolent God. Is power really evil, or can we say something about the good power, the power of God, the victory of life over death wishes? The third position attempts to think of the resurrection of Christ and our escape from death as participation in God's power.

The transition from the second to the third position is connected with my growth into the theologies of liberation. I slowly came to understand that outside the power to shout and shoot, outside the power of the imperium, there are yet other forms of power which arise out of our being bound up with the ground of life. The grass that grows into the light through the asphalt also has power: not power to command, to rule, to manipulate, but a power which comes to life from a relationship. How can we distinguish good power, the power of life, from evil power, the power to dominate? This question is central for a feminist and thus humane way of thinking. The most important criterion for answering it is that good power is shared power, power which distributes itself, which involves others, which grows through dispersion and does not become less. In this sense the resurrection of Christ is a tremendous distribution of power. The women who were the first to experience it were given a share in the power of life. It was the tremendous certainty of God which now entered their life.

In the thought of a feminist liberation theology within the first world the concept of God has taken on a new significance, in that the relationship of the omnipotent God to helpless men and women is now understood in a different way. Real relationship means that an exchange takes place and that people gain a share in the creative, good, noncompelling power of God. Above all Jewish thought has helped me to clarify this participation in God. In the Talmud the image of God in human beings is not understood as a spiritual image; rather, we are the image of God, which means that we can act like God. Just as God made clothes for Adam and Eve, so too we can clothe the naked. Just as God fed Elijah through a raven, so we too are to feed the hungry. For Christians, nothing is more false than so to stabilize the idea of God's omnipotence and human helplessness that there is no longer any exchange between the two. In that case a reified transcendence comes about instead of the *imitatio dei* which is offered us in Jewish thought.

The task of a liberating theology is to overcome just this kind of reified transcendence. Reified transcendence portrays the God who can act only as a superman, who thus acts independently, untouchably, and powerfully. I think that all three statements about the absoluteness of God — his omnipotence, omniscience, omnipresence — all three "omnis" express a fatal imperialistic tendency in theology: the power of the independent ruler. This God is in fact no more than the dream of a culture dominated by males. For me that has become clear from one of the male myths of North American popular culture. It is the dream which is entitled "Go west." The action in these films and stories usually follows the same pattern. A village is dominated by a brutal band of criminals. More and more people get murdered. The sheriff is powerless, and people no longer dare go out on the streets. One day a young man rides in; in a short time he gets the better of the villains and creates law and order. The sheriff promises him his daughter, who has fallen hopelessly in love with the handsome stranger. But the night before the wedding the cowboy saddles his horse and rides off. New adventures are waiting: greatness is not to be tied to anyone; independence is a central value. This myth is about independent male heroes who owe no one anything, who need no one, for whom mutual help, exchange, and community are secondary matters. His strengths lie in himself alone, and to this degree this primal story reflects a God who equally needs no one, a male God.

One cannot understand feminist theology as long as one believes that it is simply a change of position or an exchange of pronouns. It is in fact about another way of thinking of transcendence, of no longer understanding it independently of everything else and in terms of domination over all others but as bound into the web of life.   —TG, 185–89

FROM DOMINATION TO SOLIDARITY

Erich Fromm, in *Psychoanalysis and Religion,* distinguished between humanitarian forms of religion and authoritarian forms. The Jewish prophets, the historical Jesus, early Buddhists, and the mystics of most religions display a kind of religion that is not repressive, not based on one-sided and asymmetric dependence. This religion operates with a force that springs from the inner life of the spirit. There is one creative power in God as well as in people. Obedience presupposes duality: one who speaks and one who listens; one who knows and one who is ignorant; a ruler and those who are ruled. Religious groups that broke away from the spirit of dependency and obedience cherish different values such as mutuality and interdependence. It is precisely in the historical context of a different religion that one begins to question the social psychological implications of the father symbol and religious emphasis on obedience. The main virtue of an authoritarian religion is obedience; self-abrogation is its center of gravity. This is in sharp contrast to a humanitarian religion, where self-realization is the chief virtue and resistance to growth is the cardinal sin.

From the standpoint of social history, such an authoritarian concept of religion affirms a given society and has a stabilizing influence on its prevailing tendencies. In this context authoritarian religion discourages any willingness to aim at greater emancipation and any critical attempt to rise above the established realities — particularly when these trends base their arguments on religious grounds: God's love and righteousness are less important than God's power. Authoritarian religion leads to that infantile clinging to consolation we can observe in the sentimentality of religious art and the history of devotionalism. But this goes together with a compulsive need for order, a fear of confusion and chaos, a desire for supervision and control.

The dangers of the religious ideology of obedience do not end when religion itself loses its spell and binding power. The Nazi ideology with its antireligious leanings proves the point that after disenchantment of the world, to use Max Weber's phrase, there is still domination and unquestioned authority and obedience. It is as though the worst qualities of religion survived its form. This is even truer today in a postreligious, technocratic culture where obedience is seen not in terms of charismatic leaders but in terms of the market forces of the economy, the use of energy, and the growing militarization of societies that, without being actually engaged in war, act as if they were. Technocrats, no doubt, have long since become our priests. But even in the new situation where obedience is preferably spoken of in terms of "the rules of the game," the structural elements of authoritarian religion persist and the remaining traces of religious education prepare the increasingly areligious masses for an obedience from which all personal features based on trust and sacrifice have vanished. When religion is dying out it is precisely this rigidity that survives; it is the authoritarian bonds that mostly persist in a life understood as dominated by technocracy. The Milgram experiment at Yale many years ago showed that a vast majority of the ordinary people included in the research were quite prepared, under scientific direction, to torture innocent fellow humans with electric current — precisely the sort of inhumanity that happens in a "culture" of obedience. Obedience operates in the barbaric ethos of fascism, but also in that of technocracy.

But why do people worship a God whose supreme quality is power, not justice; whose interest lies in subjection, not mutuality; who fears equality? Fundamentalism is on the rise in many places of monotheistic religions. Judaism and Islam, as well as Christianity, have developed branches of an authoritarian religion based on blind and substanceless obedience. Religious concepts such as "being saved" or "taking Jesus as my Savior and Lord" are used without even thinking of translating them into the context of our world, as if the repetition of pious formulas could save anyone! If the concept of obedience to God is never spelled out, then it simply shores up the values of the status quo....

There is a third oppressive tradition, apart from my national and my religious identity, that made me write this book. Coming out of German Protestantism and desperately searching for meaning inside this distorted tradition, I was not so much aware of this third power of oppression. But now I think the deepest roots to struggle with in the concept of obedience are given in my sexual identity, though I did not know this at the time the book was written. It took my American friends half a dozen years to make me aware of what I felt and wrote. When I first came to this country and started to teach at Union Theological Seminary, the faculty and students asked me again and again: What has your theology to do with your being a woman? I did not know how to respond. Of course I knew of some things I intensely disliked in male theological circles — namely, the springing from one quotation to the next in their writing without the courage to use personal discourse; the almost anal obsession with footnotes, called "scientific style"; the conscious — but much worse, the unconscious — craving for orthodoxy and the shelter it offers to the professional theologian; the neglect of historical reflection in favor of glib talk about "historicity"; the failure to evaluate and reflect on praxis.

I also felt a certain lack of candor and honesty, and I sensed no need to be personally exposed to the truth of Scripture and tradition. The theological method almost always started with "Scripture tells us...." After this I expected a "but" that seldom appeared. I was angry, though I did not quite understand why. When my friends exposed to me my own latent feminism I learned to understand my anger much better. In my student years I had learned to distinguish between the God of the philosophers and the God of Abraham, Isaac, and Jacob. This was a relevant and unforgettable insight. But none of these theologians then mentioned the God of Sarah, Rebecca, and Rachel. There was silence. The "fathers of the faith" were reflected in the idea of a father in heaven, but the "mothers of the faith" were left in a limbo of obscurity. They are unremembered, forgotten — in fact, repressed. This repression not only affects 51 percent of humankind, who as a result never found their theological voice (and maybe it wouldn't have been such an obedient voice!). It also has a catastrophic affect on the way theologians who are part of the other 49 percent express themselves.

Ignoring the female component of the soul and running down everything that has a feminine flavor has done more damage to the way theologians speak and write than any assault from the secular world. This purging and impoverishing process has led to the repression of the emphatic wholeness, awareness, and integration that marked the language of the gospel. Some of the objections to the concept of obedience that are raised in this book are clearer to me now as an outcry of a woman against a so-called scientific language devoid of a sense of emotional awareness. Much of male theological language ignores the emotions of the speaking person; it is insensitive to what people experience; it has no interest and no appeal to change the world; it has no partisanship. It has a dull flatness because it leaves no room for doubt, that shadow of faith. It not only talks about obedience but also presents itself as an act of obedient talk: blind, insensitive, unimaginative, and neither reflecting nor projecting any form of Christian praxis.

A hidden feminist in me opposed this language, this virtue, and this religion. When I set out to study theology, I had no clear idea what the word "God" meant. How could anyone, given the historical situation after the Holocaust, talk about an omnipotent heavenly Being who obviously prefers to stay in the position of an observer? What was great about this God who saw and knew what happened to people in Treblinka and Buchenwald and did not intervene? Nietzsche's announcement that God is dead made a lot of sense to me, and I could describe my position as radically Christocentric. God cannot be experienced by humans. We should cling to the powerless, nondominant Christ who has nothing more to persuade us with than his love. Christ's very powerlessness constitutes an inner-personal authority; not because he begot, created, or made us are we his, but simply because his only power is love, and this love, without any weapons, is stronger than death itself.

My difficulties with the image of God as father, begetter, ruler, and manager of history grew as I began to understand more clearly what it means to be born a woman, and therefore "incomplete," and so to have to live in a patriarchal society. How could I want power to be the dominant characteristic of my life? And how could I worship a God who was only a male?

Male power, for me, is something to do with roaring, shooting, and giving orders. I do not think this patriarchal culture has done me any more damage than it has done other women. It only became increasingly obvious to me that any identification with the aggressor, the ruler, the violator, is the worst thing that can happen to a woman.

Thus I set out to find a better theological language that could eliminate the streak of domination. I was helped by the language of the mystics.

"Source of all that is good," "life-giving wind," "water of life," and "light" are all symbols of God that do not imply power of authority and do not smack of any chauvinism. In the mystical tradition there is no room for "supreme power," domination, or the denial of one's own validity. This tradition often explicitly criticizes the lord-servant relationship and has superseded the authoritarian tradition particularly in its inventive use of language.

In the mystical tradition religion means the experience of being one with the whole, of belonging together, but never of subjection. In this perspective people do not worship God because of God's power and domination. They rather want to "drown" themselves in God's love, which is the "ground" of their existence. There is a preference for symbols like "depth," "sea," and those referring to motherhood and to nature at large. Here our relationship to God is not one of obedience but of union; it is not a matter of a distant God exacting sacrifice and self-denial, but rather a matter of agreement and consent, of being at one with what is alive. And this then becomes what religion is about. When this happens solidarity will replace obedience as the dominant virtue.

My use of the word "solidarity" tells you where I moved to from this attempt to go beyond obedience. Imagination and the claim for happiness are concepts I used in that time of transition I went through. Perhaps many people in this country may not need to hear this because the pursuit of happiness is already written into their Constitution. But there are still many others for whom the Constitution was never realized, who were told to stay in their places. Women, racial and ethnic minorities, and the poor are not freed from the culture of obedience and still must travel a long way from domination to self-determination. On this long road some of my friends who were Christians dropped religion and gave up on understanding it as a means of human liberation. I sadly disagree with them. ... In this sense this book is conservative and aims to convert people to "that old-time religion." During the last years we often sang this good old spiritual and we always added some new verses: "It was good enough for Sarah, it was good enough for Mary, it was good enough for Sojourner Truth, it was good enough for Mother Jones, it was good enough for Rosa Luxembourg, and it's good enough for me."   — CD, xii–xx

> Without weapons
> Why are you so one-sided
> people often ask me
> so blind and so unilateral
> I sometimes ask in return
> are you a christian
> if you don't mind my asking
>
> And depending on the answer I remind them
> how one-sidedly and without guarantees
> god made himself vulnerable in christ
> where would we end up
> I offer for consideration
> if god insisted on bilateral agreements
> with you and me
> who welsh on treaties
> by resorting to various tricks
> where would we end up
> if god insisted on bilateral agreements
> before he acted

Then I remind them
that god didn't come in an armored car
and wasn't born in a bank
and gave up the old miracle weapons
thunder and lightning and heavenly hosts
one-sidedly
palaces and kings and soldiers
were not his way when he
decided unilaterally
to become a human being
which means to live without weapons
—WL, 58

GOD MAKES A DIFFERENCE

One of the theological questions which I had thought about for a long time was the relationship between power and love. As a woman, I quite naturally had difficulty with the idea of a mighty — indeed omnipotent — supernatural lord, who was sometimes also called Father. I was not particularly interested in being ruled and protected by a heavenly sovereign of his kind. The idea of God which had been passed down to me by the fathers of the Christian tradition seemed essentially "macho" — a man — God only for men. He was more interested in power than in anything else. Indeed he allegedly even wanted to be almighty. He was built up on the model of the free employer, who is independent of his workers. His titles — king, and so forth — insulted my democratic feelings, and the name "Lord" was an affront to my solidarity with the people who always had to live under some master or other.

It was a long time before I was able to free myself from this God; and my path led me to a nontheistic theology, centered

on the sufferings of the love of Christ. It was in this context
that I wrote my first book, *Christ the Representative*. The Son
was closer to me than the Father, because he revealed what the
Father was unable to communicate to me: love without privilege, love which empties itself and takes upon itself the form
of a servant, of a member of the proletariat, love which prefers
hell to heaven as long as other people are still condemned to be
in hell.

I have tried to talk about God in a new way. The important thing for me is not merely to change the sexist language,
by altering the pronouns we use for God. A world of female images and language can also be a world of domination
and false protection. It is more important to overcome the
inherited, substantial "machismo" in talk about God, which
means not making the bourgeois-male ideal our master. In
my view, the adoration of power, the wish for absolute independence, is catastrophic, both theologically and politically. If
today a central political goal for democrats is to achieve the co-
determination of workers and their control over what they do,
how can we endure talk about God which rests on the rejection
of democratization and self-determination? If God cannot give
up his power, we cannot trust him. If he doesn't want our liberation and our self-determination, then he is no better than, at
most, a liberal capitalist. The God whom we need is not a private owner. There is only one legitimation of power, and that
is to share it with others. Power which isn't shared — which, in
other words, isn't transformed into love — is pure domination
and oppression.

In the imprisonment of the old language, God is essentially
separated from us, in the way that masters are separated from
their servants, kings from their subjects, and independent em-
ployers from "their" workers. Our present task is to express
liberation in such a way that it doesn't take place from above

downward — that helpless objects are not just placed in some other situation by virtue of some heavenly intervention. No one can rise from the dead for anyone else; even Christ doesn't rise "for us," but only as the first among many brothers and sisters.

There are times when we feel nothing of his resurrection — times of pain and torture, times of many crosses. In spite of that, let us not be among those who suppress the news of the resurrection or no longer believe in it ourselves. In times of many crosses we should go on telling what we have heard and understood. We should talk in such a way that Christ is missed, that he is even present as someone who is missing. We should express the pain we feel when we don't perceive his victory; we should utter our longing. But to be missed is another way of being present. To have disappeared is a way of being there. Don't let us yield death an inch more than it already has. Let us talk about finding again what has disappeared, about the feeding of the hungry and about the resurrection of the dead.

In Auschwitz, from September 1943 to July 1944, there was a family concentration camp in which children lived who had been taken there from Theresienstadt and who — in order to mislead world opinion — wrote postcards. In this camp — and now comes a resurrection story — education in various forms was carried on. Children who were already destined for the gas chambers learned French, mathematics, and music. The teachers were completely clear about the hopelessness of the situation. Without a world themselves, they taught knowledge of the world. Exterminated themselves, they taught non-extermination and life. Humiliated themselves, they restored the dignity of human beings. Someone may say: "But it didn't help them." But so say the Gentiles. Let us rather say, "It makes a difference." Let us say, in terms solely of this world: "God makes a difference." —CL, 95–97

GOD IS LOVE

God and love are inseparable. It is not possible — and this is probably the gravest error of all conservative theologies — to tear God and love apart and to say that God is primary and permanent while love is some secondary, derivative thing. The gospel never tells us to believe first, then love. It describes the achievement of Christian life in terms of unity: In loving, we believe. In loving, we depend on something other than ourselves.

As you know, the many critics of the new theology complain that we preach "nothing but a little human kindness, nothing but love." And they ask if that is in fact all there really is. And if it is, what comes after death? If God and love are as closely linked as I have claimed they are, these objections amount to no more than cynicism. Faced with the reality of six million murdered Jews or the reality of a starving child, one cannot speak seriously of "nothing but a little human kindness, nothing but love," implying that these things are too little.

But since we all, at one time or another, have to number ourselves among those for whom love is too little, we have to ask what it is beyond love that we expect. What are all those people expecting who are looking for something else, who are, perhaps, faithful churchgoers or still maintain some kind of tie with the church? I suspect they are afraid. They want greater security than love offers, the land of security that can be conveyed by words like "father," "peace," "eternal rest." They want answers to their questions. Having no rest, they want rest. After war, they want to know where peace can be found. I think these needs are genuine and justified. But the gospel revises these needs for us. To all those who want a father, eternal peace, a final home, and answers to all their questions, the gospel says simply and inexorably: "All you need is love." You do not need anything else; nothing else is asked of you; nothing else counts. This is the one thing that really matters. Everything else is peripheral; we can do without it. A yearning for security and for an eternal companion is understandable. But in Christ, we are relieved of this yearning. Christ said that our eternal companion is to be found in our earthly companions and nowhere else. To live, we do not need what has repeatedly been called "God," a power that intervenes, rescues, judges, and confirms. The most telling argument against our traditional God is not that he no longer exists or that he has drawn back within himself but that we no longer need him. We do not need him because love is all we need, nothing more. We will have to develop this essential message of the gospel in terms of the tasks that face our generation and the next one after us. We will have to demonstrate concretely what love means. Questions about the nature, the degree, the spheres of influence of love will prove to be immaterial. We will be struck by the fact that love is indivisible, that it cannot be broken down into sexual love, charity, and love in the social and political realm. We know already that those who condemn the powers of sexual love make other people incapable of the love we call charity and mercy.

If there is something we will be able to say about God in the future, it will be this: God is our capacity to love. God is the power, the spark, that animates our love. When we have come far enough to understand that, we will no longer be afraid of banality. Nor will we succumb to that heresy which says Christ addresses our superegos and demands the impossible of us, for we know once again now that he has always moved our hearts. We should stop looking for God. He has been with us for a long time.   —SW, 136–38

DENYING GOD...

"The ultimate cause of our salvation lies in becoming nothing, in putting off our self." For this "I"-lessness" (which is identical to the goal of Buddhist meditation) the German mystics coined the term *Gelassenheit*. "Go out of yourself and deny yourself" (Meister Eckhart) is the oft-repeated summons to the inward journey. Such an expression was the fourteenth-century equivalent of our "turn on, tune in, drop out." The word *Gelassenheit* has undergone a drastic change in meaning over the years, a change that has diminished the mystical and strengthened the Stoic overtones of the word. The word *gelassen* has come to mean apathy, insensitivity, coldness of feeling. Henry Suso (ca. 1295–1366), a German mystic of the fourteenth century, who though he was not particularly original or outspoken was a tender and sensitive man, used the term in a much wider sense to include the ideas of patience, self-denial, obedience, conciliatoriness, acquiescence, self-control, control of desires, surrender to God. The term is used in contrast to selfishness or whatever lays emphasis upon the I and the self. A person filled with that emphasis must learn first of all to surrender himself. Indeed, this is the most important thing he can learn. He must learn no longer to cling to property, health, comfort, labor, the fruits of labor, and the lusts of the flesh. What is attempted here amounts to a radical dropout, comparable to certain phenomena of the drug culture, in which people reject the most highly cherished values of the age such as education and career, getting and spending, health and creature comforts, work and sexuality, and everything connected with these values. One must keep in mind the true picture, the countercultural point of it all, if one is to assess fairly the obvious misery of the new dependence and the ruin to which it leads.

Unless there is a radical negation of those immanent values to which the ego is enslaved, it is not possible to abolish all self-ishness and to deny oneself. "All the love in this world is based on self-love. If you had denied yourself you would have denied the entire world." In the thinking of the German mystics we can distinguish three steps in the denial of self. The first step is to deny the world, which is also called the flesh. But at the same time this denial threatens the ego, its will, and its relationships. I must also deny myself; that is the second step. I must be able to go away from myself and not worry about it. I must not cling to anything, not even to my own feelings, especially feelings of depression — and the mystics knew a great deal about such feel-ings. In this sense the expression "I am dependent upon God" has a deep meaning. I do not need to cling to these things be-cause I myself am held fast. I do not need to carry a burden because I myself am carried. I can go away from myself and deny myself. To be able to surrender myself means that I can die. Thus, I go "from life into a kind of death"; I can overcome the deepest narcissism, which, according to Freud, consists of unconsciously denying the reality of our own death and being persuaded of our own immortality. . . .

The goal of the mystics is the birth of God in the soul. As with the Greek Fathers, this means that God's becoming man is in harmony with the idea of man's becoming God. What is novel about this idea is its revolutionary implication that be-came politically explosive in the left-wing Reformation. God can be born only in the soul that is "empty," that has cast out all selfishness and has gone from ego to self. "I live, yet not I but Christ lives in me." He who has denied himself is on the way to becoming a Christ.

The third and highest step in the process of denial is that of denying not only the world and the ego but even God, the conquering One, the revealed God who promises salvation.

"Therefore I beseech God to make me have done with him."
The mystics sought to extend the limits language sets upon communication, to shrink the sphere in which silence is the only
possibility. To that end they made use of the forms of negative theology and of paradoxes ("Thou silent shout," "brilliant
darkness"). Repeatedly the mystics were accused of heresy, of
embracing radical views. That we should "deny" God for God's
sake is one such radical thought. The meaning of such a thought
is probably made clearer by Jung's assertion that religious symbols and words, the traditions about God, are supposed to act
as a buffer against the direct experience of God. The yearning
for the absolute is communicated in the religions in a variety of
ways: linguistic, social, mythical, ritual. At the same time this
means that this yearning has restricted itself and put an end to
itself. What once was faith has become a work, a pledging of
oneself to someone. "So long as you do your works for the sake
of gaining heaven or for your own salvation, that is, outwardly,
things are not well with you." The *Gelassenheit* which denies
even God destroys this circumscription.   —DBA, 81–84

. . . FOR GOD'S SAKE

The God of the German mystics appears to be a God who is
purely regressive. Their fascination with the inward journey, of
submerging oneself, is so great that it is often comparable to a
fascination with death. They appear to hold no brief for the return journey, for the life that is supposed to be new, reborn. But
this appearance is deceptive. Even Meister Eckhart was critical
of pure regression. "For in truth, if someone presumes to receive
more in spirituality, meditation, sweet rapture, and the grace of
God than at his hearth or in the animal shed, then you are acting in no way other than as if you took hold of God, threw a

cloak around his head, and tucked him under a bench." Eck-hart's verbal imagery summarizes the regressive tendency quite accurately. God is wrapped up like a baby, its head chopped off and hidden away in a hole. "For whoever seeks God in a certain way takes that way and overlooks and misses God, who is hidden in that way. But he who seeks God by no way grasps God as he is in himself, and such a person lives with the Son who is life itself." Accordingly then, regression is an essential way by which to seek God, but regression dare not be made into the absolute, into God.

Even the practice of the mystics contradicts the idea that they held solely to mere regression. Indeed, many of these same people were also quite active as leaders in their respective orders who cried out against the prevailing state of affairs in their day and age. They traveled hither and yon, preached to great crowds, and labored as teachers and as physicians of souls. They founded schools and involved themselves in ecclesiastical and court politics. Some were even placed on trial and punished. Eckhart was one of these. Such activities always had political overtones and significance because the mystics offered their theology in the language of the common people rather than in scholarly or monastic Latin. This theology gave the masses a tremendous consciousness of their own worth: they could become one with God. And the mystics proclaimed this without mention of priest and sacraments. It is impossible to understand the many reform and sectarian movements of the late Middle Ages and their theological-political demands for the abolition of private property and autocracy apart from the theology of the mystics. Thus, the most radically heretical mystics, often called "free spirits," rejected the traditional doctrines of the church dealing with creation, redemption, and eternal punishment as well as the concepts of good and evil for those who thought they had attained perfection and peace through mystical oneness with God. Their return journey contained certain new ways of life and social changes; they rejected oaths as well as priesthood, sacramentalism, and private property. Likewise they rejected all forms of government that claimed to be based on greater knowledge, clerical ordination, noble birth, or masculine gender.

For them, contemplation and action, self-submersion and politics, and religious regression and progress constituted a unity. But for our understanding there is another difficulty that accompanies the mystics' understanding of God. Their writings speak of "loving God," "seeking God," or — in paradoxical language — of "denying God for God's sake." Turning to God always means turning away from the world. This sharp delineation between God and "the world," which permeates the entire body of traditional Christian (as well as Islamic and Jewish) thought, would be wrongly understood if it were understood in terms of time and space. Neither heaven nor eternity is played off out there against earth and life, even though this Platonic idea is what is suggested. Much more is meant by "God" and "world." What is meant is a direction of will and of the existence of man. If they seek their life in contented self-assertion, in holding on, in making oneself secure, if they are bent on having, possessing, dominating, then that is what tradition calls being "of the flesh" or "of the world." If, on the other hand, the intention of life is dedication, self-denial, and self-submersion, being instead of having, giving instead of owning, communicating instead of dominating, then that is what tradition calls "seeking God." This God alone, whom one should seek, is not a separate heavenly person in a delimited, metaphysical reality that would stand only in a negative relationship to us.

God means much more from a Christian point of view. To put it simply, God always means "love" and world always

means "not love," which expresses itself as anxiety, detach-
ment, security, "I-ness." In no case does the term "world" mean
human beings, what the modern age calls mankind; the human
being in this understanding belongs much more on the side of
God. When reference is made to seeking "something" and not
"God," this does not imply a distancing from one's neighbor
but only a distancing from whatever dehumanizes, making a
thing of a human being who no longer values other people
but only the possession of things. The distinction between "this
world" and "God" is the attempt to draw human beings over
to the side of God.   —DBA, 88–90

A MYSTICAL JOURNEY FOR TODAY

[Matthew] Fox's way and that of traditional mysticism differ
in two aspects. The first is where the way of mysticism is said
to begin. In the understanding of mysticism inherited from the
Neoplatonists Proclus and Plotinus, purging or purification is
always the first step. The beginning of mystical piety is not the
beauty and goodness of creation but the fall of human beings
from paradise. That this loaded word "fall" does not appear
in the Hebraic narrative of the expulsion from paradise seems
not to be known. Instead, in this context, marked strongly by
Augustine, there is little talk of creation, of the cosmos, and
its original goodness. But does this not place the mystical journey at far too late a point in the course of the Christian history
of redemption? One of the basic questions Fox asks again and
again is whether we ought not refer first of all to the blessing of
the beginning, that is, not to original sin but to original blessing? And is it not exactly mystical experience that points us to
creation and the good beginning?

The second difference in comparison to the Western tradition of mysticism has to do with the vision of union with God. I agree with Fox on the matter of the *via unitiva*. He defines the goal of the journey differently in this stage; it is more world-related. The goal is creativity and compassion. Creativity presupposes union with the Creator, whose power lives in the oneness with us. Today we understand creativity not only as the transformation of an individual soul but of the world as a whole, in which humans could live together. To speak of this *via transformativa* means to embed the mystical project in the context of our life, which is marked by the catastrophe of economic and ecological exploitation.

For me, mysticism and transformation are indissolubly interconnected. Without economic and ecological justice (known as ecojustice) and without God's preferential love for the poor and for this planet, the love for God and the longing for oneness seem to me to be an atomistic illusion. The spark of the soul acquired in private experience may, indeed, serve the search for *gnosis* (knowledge) in the widest sense of the word, but it can do no more. A genuine mystical journey has a much larger goal than to teach us positive thinking and to put to sleep our capacity to be critical and to suffer.

As in the journeys of former times, the stages of today's journey flow one into the other. The three stages are as follows: to be amazed, to let go, and to resist. The first step taken on the way of mysticism is amazement. I relate an experience by way of example: When my oldest son was learning to read numbers, he stood still one day in front of a house's number plate and did not move an inch. When I wanted to move him on with my "come on!" he said, "Look, Mummy, what a wonderful 537!" Naturally, I had never seen it. He spoke the number slowly, tasting it in a mood of discovery. He was submerged in happiness.

I think that every discovery of the world plunges us into jubilation, a radical amazement that tears apart the veil of triviality. Nothing is to be taken for granted, least of all beauty!

The first step of this mystical way is a *via positiva*, and it occurs in the primordial image of the rose that blooms in God. The jubilation of my five-year-old responds to the experience of "radical amazement," as Abraham Heschel (1907–72) calls this origin of our being-in-relation. Without this overwhelming amazement in the face of what encounters us in nature and in history's experiences of liberation, without beauty experienced even on a busy street and made visible in a blue-and-white number plate on the wall of a house, there is no mystical way that can lead to union. To be amazed means to behold the world and, like God after the sixth day of creation, to be able to say again or for the first time, "Look! How very good it all is!"

But it is not enough to describe this amazement as an experience of bliss alone. Amazement also has its bleak side of terror and hopelessness that renders one mute. The ancient Greeks already defended themselves against this bleakness by an injunction against adoring things; Horace summed it up in his motto *nihil admirari* (admire nothing). But this prohibition, with the help of which scientific thinking once was supposed to banish the fear of fear, has succeeded in banishing the demons together with all the angels. Gone is the sensation of paralyzing fright together with the ability to be marvelously amazed. Those who seek to leave behind the terrifying, sinister side of wonderment, the side that renders us dumb, take on, through rational superiority, the role of those who own the world. In my view, to be able to own and to be amazed are mutually exclusive. "What would it help someone, if he gained the whole world but damaged his soul?" (Matt. 16:26, in Luther's German translation).

The soul needs amazement, the repeated liberation from customs, viewpoints, and convictions, which, like layers of fat that make us untouchable and insensitive, accumulate around us. What appears obvious is that we need to be touched by the spirit of life and that without amazement and enthusiasm nothing new can begin. Goethe's friend Herder said that "without enthusiasm nothing great and good ever came to be in this world. Those who were said to be 'enthusiasts' have rendered humankind the most useful services." This is exactly the point where the Christian religion — in a world that makes it possible for us human beings, through science, to create cosmic consciousness while, at the same time, through technology, also to undo creation — must learn anew from its own origin in the tradition of Judaism.

What this means in relation to where the journey takes its beginning is that we do not set out as those who seek but as those who have been found. The goodness we experience is there already long before. In an ontological and not necessarily a chronological sense, before the prayers of those who feel abandoned and banished there is the praise without which they would not perceive themselves as banished ones. This ability for wonderment brings about consenting to one's being here, being today, being now. "Being here is magnificent" (Rainer Maria Rilke). Like every form of ecstasy, this ability implies a self-forgetfulness that, as if by magic, lifts us out of ordinary self-forgetfulness and its corresponding triviality.

Amazement or wonderment is a way of praising God, even if God's name is not mentioned. In amazement, whether we know it or not, we join ourselves to the heavens "who declare the glory of the Eternal One" (Ps. 19:1). "The beginning of our happiness lies in the understanding that life without wonder is not worth living." Such an understanding of the wonder of

being is not dependent on whether the origin of creation is con-
ceived of in personal terms, as in the Abrahamic religions, or
in nonpersonal ones. Radical amazement does not have to atro-
phy as scientific knowledge increases and better explains what
is; on the contrary, such amazement grows in the finest scientific
minds who frequently feel attracted to mysticism.

Can amazement, the radical wonderment of the child, be
learned again? Whatever the badly misused word "meditation"
means, it embraces a form of stopping and tarrying wherein individuals or communities intentionally set aside for themselves
times and places other than the ordinary ones. Listening, being
still, at rest, contemplating, and praying are all there to make
room for amazement. "Hear this, O Job, stop and consider the
wondrous works of God" (Job 37:14). The unknown name of
the mystical rose reminds us of our own amazed blissfulness.

The practice of amazement is also a beginning in leaving
oneself; it is a different freedom from one's own fears. In amazement we detrivialize ourselves and enter the second stage of
the mystical journey, that of letting go. If to praise God is
the first prompting of the journey, then to miss God is another unavoidable dimension of it. The more profound the
amazed blissfulness of the *sunder warumbe* (the utter absence
of any why or wherefore), the darker the night of the soul (*via
negativa*). The tradition that most often places this way of purification at the beginning and points out ever new ways of
asceticism, renunciation, and escape from desires also teaches
to discern how far one is from the true life in God.

Letting go begins with simple questions: What do I perceive?
What do I keep away from myself? What do I choose? We need
a bit of "un-forming" or liberation before we, in the language
of Suso, can be "con-formed" to Christ or transformed. In the
world ruled by the media, this "un-forming" has yet a wholly
other status than it had in the rural and monastic world of

the Middle Ages when life was so much less subject to diversions. For us who today know a hitherto undreamed abundance of available consumer goods and artificially manufactured new needs, this stage of the journey plays a different role than it does in the cultures of want. We associate rituals of purification and fasting most frequently with such puritanical "giving-up" performances alleged to be necessary in the development of industrial labor morality. In postindustrial consumer society, this ethics works less and less. Our letting go is related above all to our growing dependency on consumerism. We need purification (*purgatio*), both in the coercive mechanisms of consumption and in the addictions of the everyday working world.

The more we let go of our false desires and needs, the more we make room for amazement in day-to-day life. We also come closer to what ancient mysticism called "being apart," which is living out concretely one's farewell to the customs and norms of one's culture. Precisely the fact that our mysticism begins not with banishment but with amazement is what makes the horror about the destruction of wonder so radical. Our relation to the basic realities of ownership, violence, and the self is changing. In this turning away from our rough ways (*Entgröbung*), the road becomes increasingly narrower. Companions and friends take their leave and the initial amazement clouds over. The symbol of the first stage of mysticism's path is the rose, that of the second stage is the dark night.

To miss God is a form of tradition called "suffering from God." To become more and more empty means not only to jettison unnecessary ballast but also to become more lonely. Given the destruction of nature that marks our context, it becomes more and more difficult to turn back to certain forms of our relationship to and with nature and to the original amazement. Mystical spirituality of creation will very likely move deeper and deeper into the dark night of being delivered into the hands of the principalities and powers that dominate us. For it is not only the poor man from Nazareth who is tortured together with his brothers and sisters on the cross, it is also our mother earth herself.

The horizon of ecological catastrophe is the backdrop before which today's road of the mystical journey has to be considered. To praise God *and* to miss nothing so much as God leads to a "life in God" that the tradition called the *via unitiva*. To become one with what was intended in creation has the shape of *co-creation;* to live in God means to take an active part in the ongoing creation.

The third stage leads into a healing that is at the same time resistance. The two belong together in our situation. Salvation means that humans live in compassion and justice co-creatively; in being healed (saved) they experience also that they can heal (save). In a manner comparable to how Jesus' disciples understood themselves to be "healed healers," so every way of union is one that continues onward and radiates outward. Being-at-one is not individualistic self-realization but moves beyond that to change death-oriented reality. Being-at-one shares itself and realizes itself in the ways of resistance. Perhaps the most powerful symbol of this mystical oneness is the rainbow, which is the sign of the creation that does not perish but continues to live in sowing and harvesting, day and night, summer and winter, birth and death.

BEING AMAZED	LETTING GO	HEALING / RESISTING
via positiva	*via negativa*	*via transformativa*
radical amazement	being apart	changing the world
bliss	letting go of possession, violence, and ego	compassion and justice
praising God	missing God	living in God
the rose	the "dark night"	the rainbow

—SC, 88–93

UNITY

Mysticism creates a new relation to the three powers that, each in its own totalitarian way, hold us in prison: the ego, possession, and violence. Mysticism relativizes them, frees us from their spell, and prepares us for freedom. Those powers project themselves in very diverse ways. The ego that keeps on getting bigger presents itself most often as well-mannered and civilized, even when it seeks to get rid of every form of ego-lessness. Possession, which according to Francis of Assisi makes for a condition that forces us to arm ourselves, appears in a neutralized, unobtrusive form. The fact that the very entities with which we destroy creation — namely, possession, consumption, and violence — have fashioned themselves into a unity in our world makes no impact, whether by design or through ignorance.

When women like Dorothy Day are not fixated on their own egos, or when fools without possessions, like some of Saint Francis's sons and daughters, live different, liberated lives, they are met with smiles of derision. But when they dare to take real steps out of the violence-shaped actuality of our condition, they come into conflict with the judiciary or wind up in jail. More than anything else, violence must hide itself and always put on new garments, disguising itself in the form of imperatives, such as security, protection, technological necessity, public order, or defensive measures.

Here is an inconspicuous example. In June 1997, a member of the White Fathers, a religious community that is part of the "Order for Peace," was fined for having demonstrated outside the chancellor's office in Bonn with a picket sign saying "Cancel Third World Debts." The office had refused to accept a petition, signed by twelve thousand people, sponsored by the campaign "Development Needs Forgiveness of

Debts." The harmless name of the violence behind which the chancellor's office was hiding is the law of inviolable precincts; under present circumstances it is one of the many, actually quite sensible garments of state power. But the law is abused when the office of state protects itself against democratic interventions and expects submission to or passivity in face of economic violence rather than a decisive No! of noncooperation.

This rather insignificant example of civil disobedience illustrates how people make use of violence. For many it is no longer good enough to behave nonviolently in their personal lives and to submit to administrative regulations. For in such "nonviolence" and submission, as the powerful of this world define them, the real violence that renders the countries of the third world destitute is left untouched. To exist free of violence means much more than that: it means to think and act with other living beings in a common life. These forms of the freedom of opposition and resistance have multiplied in the last centuries also in Europe in the face of the militaristic and technocratic coercion. An essential and new role is played here by the basic insights of mysticism, such as those of the tradition of Gandhi as well as the Quakers.

In the eighties I was occasionally asked, especially within the contexts of civil disobedience against nuclear arms, whether I did not sense something in myself of the power and spirit of the other, the enemy: "Where is the Ronald Reagan in you?" I was in no mood to respond with a speculation about my shadow side. I do not think that a pacifist has to be complemented by a bellicist. Perhaps I did not understand correctly the seriousness of the question that seeks to grasp the unity of all human beings; to me the question seemed intent on neutralizing or mollifying what we were about. When I ask myself seriously what the principalities and powers that rule over me as structural powers claim from me, the answer is that it is my own cowardice that they seek to make use of. Those who submit to those powers also are part of the violence under whose velvet terror we live and destroy others.

Before he found his way to nonviolent resistance, Gandhi used to describe that time by saying that it was as a coward that he accommodated himself to violence. I understand this in a twofold sense. First, I submitted to external violence, which is to say I knuckled under, paid my taxes with which more weapons were produced, I followed the advice of my bank, and I consumed as the advertisers commanded. Worse still, I hankered after violence, wanted to be like "them" in the advertisements, as successful, attractive, aesthetic, and intelligent as they were. The existential step that the word nonviolence signals leads out of the forced marriage between violence and cowardice. And that means in practice that one becomes unafraid of the police and the power of the state.

The forms of resistance that revoke the common consensus about how we destroy creation have deep roots in a mysticism that we often do not recognize as such. It is the mysticism of being at one with all that lives. One of the basic mystical insights in the diverse religions envisions the unity of all human beings, indeed, of all living beings. It is part of the oldest wisdom of religion that life is no individual and autonomous achievement. Life cannot be made, produced, or purchased, and is not the property of private owners. Instead, life is a mystery of being bound up with and belonging one to another. Gandhi believed that he could live a spiritual life only when he began to identify himself with the whole of humankind, and he could do that only by entering into politics. For him the entire range of all human activities is an indivisible whole. Social, economic, political, and religious concerns cannot be cultivated in sterile plots that are hermetically sealed off from one another. To bring

those sterile, sealed-off plots together in a related whole is one
of the aims of the mysticism whose name is resistance.

—SC, 259–61

"SUCCESS IS NOT A NAME OF GOD"

How do we become free of the ego? In the twentieth century,
Simone Weil provided a new instruction in preparing oneself
for this work. In her endeavors she took up the notion of "attention," perhaps from Buddhism. In one of her most beautiful
essays, which deals with "a Christian conception of studies,"
she combines school and university studies, generally associated with scholarly, scientific thinking, with the mystical sense
of dedication that integrates and focuses us. "If we concentrate
our attention on trying to solve a problem of geometry, and if
at the end of an hour we are no nearer to doing so than at
the beginning, we have nevertheless been making progress each
minute of that hour in another more mysterious dimension.
Without our knowing or feeling it, this apparently barren effort
has brought more light into the soul. The result will one day be
discovered in prayer." Simone Well explicitly brings attention
and prayer together. "The quality of the attention counts for
much in the quality of the prayer." Every exercise directed to
our ability to be attentive changes us inasmuch as it diverts us
from focusing on the self. "Even if our efforts of attention seem
for years to be producing no result, one day a light that is in
exact proportion to them will flood the soul." From this sort of
understanding that hovers between concentration and attention
a new freedom from the ego can emerge. It is perhaps the greatest step in the "un-forming" that Heinrich Seuse speaks of in
his mystical journey toward the "acquiescing" human being. It
is preconditional for being "conformed to the image of Christ,"

which Simone Weil regards as the preparation for prayer. "Students must...work without any wish to gain good marks, to pass examinations, to win school successes; without any reference to their natural abilities and tastes, applying themselves equally to all their tasks with the idea that each one will help to form them in the habit of that attention which is the substance of prayer." The purpose-free nature of Eckhart's *sunder warumbe* can hardly be put more clearly. "Attention consists in suspending our thought, leaving it detached, empty, and ready to be penetrated by the object." In this emptiness something evil in oneself is unintentionally destroyed and a kind of inattentiveness disappears. Simone Weil makes use of the beautiful examples of writers' work in which one enters upon "a way of waiting...for the right word to come of itself at the end of our pen, while we merely reject all inadequate words."

To reject the inadequate, not to be satisfied with it, is mystical activity. Emptiness is a better condition for the soul than being flooded with orientations that turn the ego into a helpmate of destructive reality. In rejecting inadequate words, we also reject inadequate feelings, images, conceptions, and desires so that in true prayer false desires vanish and others, greater and perhaps more mute ones, arise. Here the classical philosophical distinction between activity and passivity is abolished. The ego becoming free acts and, at the same time, lets itself be acted upon.

What do ego-lessness and becoming unattached mean in connection with today's mystical way in the form of resistance? Concepts like asceticism, renunciation of consumerism, and using less and simpler ways of living make it apparent that the way of conscious resistance has to lead from ego-fixation (that globalized production requires as a partner) to ego-lessness. What is missing is a reflection that shows more clearly how complicit we are ourselves in the consumerist ego that the economy desires. I want to elucidate this in terms of a question that every nonconformist group, every critical minority wishing to contribute to the establishment of a different life has to face, namely, the question of success.

Decisions about possible actions are weighed in a world governed by market considerations by one and only one criterion: success. Is it necessary now to boycott certain aspects of consumerism, to blockade nuclear waste transports, to hide refugees threatened with repatriation, or offer pacifist resistance against further militarization? Whenever such topics are raised, questions like the following are regularly heard: "What's the use of protesting, everything has been decided long ago?" "Can anything be changed anyway?" "What do you think you will accomplish?" "Whom do you want to influence?" "Who is paying attention?" "Will the media report it?" "How much publicity will it have?" "Do you really believe that this can succeed?" Sadly and helplessly, many people say; "I am with you, but this symbolic or real action is of no use against the concentrated power of the others." Questions and responses like these nourish doubt in democracy, but worse, they jeopardize partiality for life. Behind questions like these lurks a cynicism that shows how powerfully the ego is tied into conditions and relations of power.

Martin Buber said that "success is not a name of God." It could not be said more mystically nor more helplessly. The nothing that wants to become everything and needs us cannot be named in the categories of power. (That is why the "omnipotent" God is a male, helpless, and antimystical metaphor that is void of any responsibility.) To let go of the ego means, among other things, to step away from the coercion to succeed. It means to "go where you are nothing." Without this form of mysticism, resistance loses it focus and dies before our very eyes. It is not that creating public awareness, winning fellow participants, and changing how we accept things is beside the point. But the ultimate criterion for taking part in actions of resistance and solidarity cannot be success because that would mean to go on dancing to the tunes of the bosses of this world.

To become ego-less, unattached, and free also involves dismissing the agent of power within us who wants to persuade us that given the huge power of institutions, resisting has no chance of succeeding. To become unattached means, in addition, to correct the relation of success and truth.

I use my own experiences from the years of the German peace movement to elucidate the point. I assumed, with a certain naiveté, that the questions journalists put to me were motivated by an interest in truth. I thought it important to find out whether particular nuclear bombs could be used for defense apart from exclusive use in first-strike offensives. I wanted to have figures showing what armaments cost and then to relate this to what those moneys could do for the education and healthcare of children. I believed that the connection between arming ourselves and letting people starve was what had to be made known. And I assumed that those who asked me questions were also interested in such often concealed truths.

It took years before I understood that the majority of media representatives had quite different interests. They did not want to know and write about who the victims of arming ourselves are; they "covered" demonstrations and protesters only from the perspective of securing viewers for that evening's news telecast. The interest in success, asking questions such as "who are you anyway and whom or what do you represent?" had increasingly superceded interest in truth. Attempts to revive an interest in truth, to make the victims visible instead of mindlessly orienting oneself to the winners, had little chance. Long years of mass movements for a peace no longer constructed on arms, for economic justice and solidarity, and for the integrity of creation have not succeeded. Discouragement over this is a bitter and undeniable reality.

Is what Bonhoeffer called "shoving a spoke in the wheel" something that we can do at all today? Mysticism of ego-lessness helps me deal with God's defeats in this world. To get rid of the ego means not to sacrifice truth to the mentality of success, to become unattached and not to uphold success as the ultimate criterion. An Italian mystic of the fourteenth century, at one time a wealthy cloth merchant, let himself and his companions be bound and driven with blows and insults through the streets where once he made his money. Just as Christ had been regarded as a madman, so these friends of God wanted to be regarded as fools and idiots (*pazzi e stolti*).

Something of this foolishness is found in many forms of organized resistance. Women are met with rudeness and invective when they hold vigils for tortured prison inmates. To become free from the coercion of compulsory success is a mystical seed that is not always at the fore of consciousness but that does sprout precisely in the defiance of "keeping on keeping on." A slogan was coined in the anti–nuclear energy movement that reflects some of this defiance of ego-lessness, *Wer sich nicht wehrt, lebt verkehrt* (the person who does not put up a fight, lives a wrong life). A Hassidic rabbi puts it in more pious language. Maintaining steadfast in prayer, he said: "and if you don't want to redeem Israel yet then redeem the goyim alone."

There are many mystical teachers who can help in satisfactorily reaching the point of no return with what they teach us concerning the unattached ego, about going out of ourselves, and about freedom from constraint. Thomas Merton, a Trappist monk and a leading opponent of the Vietnam War, wrote about the mystical foundation of this freedom in a letter to James Forest in 1966: "Do not depend on the hope of results. When you are doing the sort of work you have taken on, essentially an apostolic work, you may have to face the fact that your work will be apparently worthless and even achieve no result at all, if not perhaps results opposite to what you expect. As you get used to this idea, you start more and more to concentrate not on the results but on the value, the rightness, the truths of the work itself." He advises the younger pacifist to become free from the need to find his own affirmation. For then "you can be more open to the power that will work through you without your knowing it." Living in mystical freedom one can say then with Eckhart, "I act so that I may act." Being at one with creation represents a conversion to the ground of being. And this conversion does not nourish itself from demonstrable success but from God.

Years ago, American friends persuaded me that the best way to remember the infanticide of Bethlehem, when King Herod ordered all children under the age of two to be killed (Matt. 2:16–18), was for peace activists to go to the Pentagon on the second day of Christmas, which is dedicated to the remembrance of those innocent children, and pour blood on the white pillars there in order to give witness to what is planned and commanded there. I went along, but with many doubts. Was it only a gesture, a kind of theatrical production? What success would it achieve? The clearer that question became to me, the more astounded I was that my friends in this mystical peace movement, shaped by the Catholic Worker movement..., had left this question behind them. They had become free of it and their freedom seemed greater to me than my own.   —SC, 228–32

EVERYTHING DEPENDED ON THEM

To which God are we really speaking? At a conference there was a group of women conversing about religious questions.

One asked where God had been at Auschwitz. A young woman from the evangelical camp, who described herself as a believer, answered with the sentence: "Auschwitz was willed by God." Everyone was appalled and wanted to know how she meant that. "Quite simply," she said, "if God had not willed it, it would not have happened. Nothing happens without God." The Wholly Other God has so determined it, and though we cannot understand it we must accept it in humility. God's authority, lordship, and omnipotence may not be placed in doubt, it is not for us to inquire after God's providential will. The God who is completely independent from all God's creatures has willed everything that happens. God and God alone could have hindered it. But God's ways are not our ways. This manner of speaking about God sounds pious, but it doesn't really get anyone anywhere. It solidifies hierarchical thinking into authorities and power. It makes us into impotent nobodies on whose lives nothing actually depends. In reality *everything* depended on the lives and behavior of people in Germany for the victims of our actions. In reality everything relating to the preservation of this earth depends on the lives and behavior of people in the rich world. We are involved; we are responsible. The belief of the young fundamentalist woman is in fact not very different from the apocalyptic doomsday belief of my taxi driver.* In both modes of thinking our role as victims of an inscrutable giant machine is the same. . . . Submission without a say in the matter is common to both. Both are fixated on power and cannot think in terms of shared power, which we can also call love. For the young woman God is the sovereign Lord who would have intervened from above, had God so willed. Since God did not intervene, God must

*See p. 179.

have willed Auschwitz. The most important thing about God is God's power.

I am reminded by this way of thinking about God of a cheeky song from Vienna, in which a young man from a wealthy home carries out all possible mischief at the expense of others and then in the refrain sings reassuringly: "Papa will set things right." Many believers have never gone beyond this childish image of God; they have never learned to assume responsibility themselves. Their relationship to God remains childish; they do not want to be friends of God but want to remain subordinates and dependents.

But must we really speak in this way? God is mighty, we are helpless — is that all? A few years ago I had a meeting in a church congregation near Hamburg in which we recalled *Kristallnacht,* the night when Jewish homes, businesses, and synagogues were vandalized in 1938, prefiguring and inaugurating the full terror of the Holocaust. A woman turned up and introduced herself as an outsider. She told how she had struggled for years with the Jewish-Christian problem because she wanted to know how it came to the point of Shoah, the extermination of European Jews. She ended her contribution with the words, "When I had understood Auschwitz, I joined the peace movement." In this statement I found a different God from the omnipotent Lord of heaven and earth who is completely independent of us. This woman had understood that in the Nazi period in Germany God was small and weak. God was in fact powerless because God had no friends, male or female. God's spirit had no place to live; God's sun, the sun of righteousness, did not shine. The God who needs people in order to come into being was a nobody.

This woman did not look up to heaven in order to be comforted by an Almighty Father. She looked within and around herself. She found "that of God," as the Quakers often say, in herself, the strength for resistance, the courage for a clear no in a world that is drunk on the blood of the innocent. And she found another gift of the Spirit, the help of other brothers and sisters. She was not alone. She did not submit herself to a God who was falsely understood as fate. Nor did she consider living without God and in complete assimilation to the values of this world — career, prestige, income. Instead she held firm to the God who is in us as the power of liberation. Her God was small, a minority, laughable, politically suspect and, from a pragmatic viewpoint, unsuccessful. God is practically irrelevant for the great majority precisely because of God's noninterference. But God is (to use an expression of American theologians) no "interventionist," who interferes by intervening, but an "intentionist," who makes the divine will and intention discernible. I could simply say: God dreams us, even today.

But, I hear someone object, doesn't this way of speaking about God only make sense if God embodies some kind of power? If something in our lives changes through and with God? Who is this God who has caused a woman not to let Auschwitz rest, not to let fate be fate, not to give way to the ordinary fatalism of subordination to the wolves that howl the loudest. Does such a God have any kind of power, then, or is this form of divinity as powerless in the face of the forces that control us as any child in Bethlehem? I think the question whether God is the one who holds everything in hand and can intervene or whether God is small under the forces of this world cannot be decided rationally, but rather existentially. "When I had understood Auschwitz, I joined the peace movement." That is to say: I did not rid myself of God like many who had handed over responsibility to God alone; rather I grasped that God needs us in order to realize what was intended in creation. God dreams us, and we should not let God dream alone. In the words of a Latin American song:

> One day the earth will belong to all people
> and the people will be free
> as you, God, have willed it
> from the very beginning.

This song speaks *to* God, not *about* God. It liberates us from the idol of fate in whose power everything happens simply as it happens. It binds us together with God who is not the all-powerful conqueror but stands instead on the side of the poor and disadvantaged — a God who is always hidden in the world and wants to become visible.   — TS, 13–17

PEACE, NOT SECURITY

If we really want peace, we must begin disarming where we are on one side, which is neither better nor worse than the other side, but has the advantage of being our side. It is rationalistic stupidity to suppose that mutual death threats can be abolished from the world through a kind of business deal. Both partners give a little, and then we have a nice balance again. Those are deceptive hopes, nourished by the idea of security and constituting a betrayal of any real hope of peace. Change can happen only when one of the partners to the conflict begins to relinquish his or her threatening attitude and makes a tiny step forward alone. Unilateralism contains an existential moment when the rationalism of business sense is abandoned. Change happens at the level of action that contains risk.

The illusion of bourgeois concepts of security lies, I think, in the expectation that peace can come from business dealings, from rational agreement. Behind this idea lies a rationalistic optimism that flies in the face of the genuine despair of peoples subjected to the ideology of security. The history of religions —

I include here the history of the nonviolent martyrs like Martin Luther King, Steve Biko, and Oscar Romero — teaches a very different lesson. It says: It doesn't happen without victims. It doesn't happen without risk. Life that excludes and protects itself against death protects itself to death. If the "window of vulnerability," as it is called in military language, is finally closed and walled up, the supposedly secure people inside the fortress will die for lack of light and air. Only life that opens itself to the other life that risks being wounded or killed contains promise. Those who arm themselves are not only killers; they are already dead.

One of the U.S. peace movement's posters shows a kind of altar standing in a desert landscape. The altar is built on three steps. On top of it stands a bomb, with its nose pointing to the skies; people kneel around it in adoration. The scene is a copy of the biblical story of the golden calf: the bomb is the golden calf from whom the people beg security.

The Reformers' tradition teaches that people always have some kind of god because there is always something they "fear and love above all things" (Luther). Even atheists have a god in this sense, to whom they bring sacrifices, for whom they work, and from whom they expect security. The correct theological question is thus not whether someone lives with or without a god, but rather which god is worshiped and adored in a particular society. Under the sign of global militarization, as it is now being practiced in and from the Western world, the God-question is easily answered: The god of "this world" is the bomb.

The bomb as symbol has a variety of meanings, on different levels of relevance for our culture. It has an economic meaning, especially evident in the analysis of the connection between militarization and underdevelopment. At the request of the United

Nations, a study was prepared showing the negative consequences of armaments for the developing nations. This research
report, completed for the 1982 special session of the UN on
disarmament, treated the interconnection of weapons, development, and global security. The document is often referred to
as the Thorsson Report, after Inge Thorsson, who directed the
research. It considers how financial resources, raw materials,
energy, and human work are put to use for military purposes.
The balance of the report, in light of the never-ending demands
of the military sector, is devastating. Appended to the report
is a list of products needed by the developing nations in those
sectors necessary to sustain life: agriculture, production and distribution of energy, medicine, transportation, and the like. All
these products could be manufactured and effect real changes in
those countries if military industry were converted to peaceful
purposes.

The calf in Israel's history was made of gold. It was a symbol
of security and welfare. As the calf was forged from the people's
jewelry and ornaments, the Israelites said: "This is your God,
O Israel who brought you up out of the land of Egypt" (Exod.
32:4). When I listen to the courtly speeches of West German
politicians, I hear them saying exactly the same thing: it is the
bomb that protects us from the Communists and brings us prosperity, security, and power. Whoever wants to retain prosperity
and security must adore the bomb and must fear, love, and trust
it above all things.

The bomb as symbol has another meaning in the field of science. In 1980, 42 percent of all scientists and engineers in the
United States were doing military work. In their research and
development of new means of mass destruction they are, often
without knowing it, adoring the bomb. On a world scale, the
majority of all individual projects in scientific research and technological development are devoted to military purposes. That

also means that the majority of scientists and technicians, immersed in their adoration of the bomb, are completely out of touch with reality. Millions of people lack both clean water and the technologies to make water usable. Millions are without shelter and have no technical means for making houses out of the local raw materials. Millions are starving and have not learned how to produce nourishing food where they live. But science, untouched by the real suffering of humanity, persists in its fascination with death and seeks to create more and better instruments for killing.

The bomb-symbol also has sexual significance, and not only because of its shape. In patriarchal culture, the man's sexual potency is thought to be connected not only with happiness, but also with violence. The German word *Vergewaltigung* for rape (*Gewalt* means force or violence) clearly expresses the fact that men can experience sex as violence, conquest, humiliation, and degradation of other persons. The golden calf was, from its origins in the Canaanite cult, really a golden steer. The adoration of the bomb is adoration of violence in every form.

The women's movement has repeatedly uncovered the connections between male dominance and war, between maleness and self-identification with the warrior, between lust and violence. The adoration of bombs made by men is only logical in this sense: In a culture that defines the human as a man and makes of woman an unknown, publicly invisible, irrelevant being, the bomb, which is the ultimate weapon, must necessarily become the most important cultural symbol. Just as the desire for security does not rise above the moral level of the bourgeoisie, so also the political culture of the present, whose heart and soul are fixed on the bomb, cannot surpass the level of the men who are its rulers. The bomb prohibits any kind of transcendence. It is God, the final, unquestionable reality. The precedence that so-called defense takes over all other political interests makes that quite obvious. In the day-to-day speeches of politicians who serve the military we can clearly hear the refrain: "You shall have no other gods besides me." Defense takes absolute precedence before all other political and social priorities.

In this sense the symbol of the bomb has religious meaning. If I am correct in my observation that political conflicts are becoming more and more obviously religious, that they more and more clearly express absolutely different worldviews, that they are less and less capable of being liberally smoothed over and rationalized, then the bomb is in fact the god of "this world." The people who adore the bomb carry it within themselves and feel themselves secure in its shadow.

In Toronto, Canada, there is a Center for Culture and Technology that collects and continues the work of philosopher and communications theorist Marshall McLuhan, who died in 1980. Dr. Derrick de Kerckhove, director of the McLuhan Program, recently expressed the idea that the atomic bomb, considered as a medium of information, was a good thing. He said in support of the stationing of new nuclear missiles in Europe: "I'm absolutely delighted the bomb is there. It's about time we had something to bring us together." The essential thought of this successor of McLuhan was that the bomb is a modern myth holding power over the culture's thinking similar to that formerly possessed by religion. "That myth has become a physical part of everyone's brain and is now acting as a strong unifying force." The bomb is "the ultimate information medium ... the more bombs the better!" De Kerckhove "is sorry that [Pershing 11 and Cruise missiles] are not widely distributed in public places, such as markets." The bomb is a universal myth; "it ... binds people together in a way they have not been linked since the Middle Ages" (*New York Times*, February 12, 1984). It is clear that, as far as McLuhan's successor is concerned, the bomb will not be used. Disarmament is therefore unnecessary. The medium is the message.

I mention this because I consider it more than intellectual nonsense. It is in fact the intellectual and scientific expression of the religion that militarism is propagating on earth. The real, practical adoration of the bomb has found its ideology. One characteristic of this religion is that it cannot distinguish God from Satan. That is also true of the fundamentalists who predict the end of the world as God's will and promote it through their politics. God, for them, is neither love nor justice, but pure power. Militarization of the whole world is the accomplishment of this God: strength is his highest ideal, violence his method, and security his promise.

The peace movement has freed itself from this god. That liberation involves a "conversion": turning away from false life, turning toward another form of life. In recent years I have again and again met people who have told me, with tears in their eyes, that they have been only "involved" in the peace movement for a few months, and that it has changed their whole lives. "Now I know why I am here." Those are the conversions that are happening, in huge numbers, before our eyes: the turning from a violent society to a peaceful one in which conflicts are carried through bloodlessly and without weapons. The image the Bible uses for this conversion is drawn entirely from materials and technology. It does not speak simply of a change of heart, but rather of a conversion of the armaments industry to a peaceful industry: swords into plowshares.

Thanks to the massive disruption, or rather destruction, of religion by the dominant churches in our country, many people do not even know that the conversion from security to peace is the most important religious event in their lives — just as our bishops fail to comprehend that people are seeking God when they fasten stickers proclaiming "Fight Atomic Death" on the doors of their houses. When they do this, they have converted the bourgeois desire for security, mediated by possessions and property, into the universal longing for peace, a desire that includes the other members of the human family as well and that is mediated by another way of being, namely, being for others.

This is only a start. Someday this movement will be so strong, so unmistakable, so ready to renounce and to suffer, that everyone will be able to see the other God within it. Today it is plain that whoever continues to arm some people is working toward the death of all. Why did God make us as weaponless beings in the first place? The movement to disarm the human being is just beginning.   — WV, 7–11

A SPIRITUALITY OF CREATION

In my own search for a new language of celebration, I am struck by the fact that verbs, not nouns, spring to mind. I need to wonder, to be amazed, to be in awe, to renew myself in the rhythm of creation, to perceive its beauty, to rejoice in creation, and to praise the source of life. Listing these verbs reminds me of people who believe that God has created them and all creatures, who trust in the goodness of creation. I cannot forget, however, all my brothers and sisters who have never learned to wonder, to be amazed, to renew themselves, and to rejoice. I think of those whose experiences do not lead to a deep trust and a belief in the goodness of creation. In German there is a colloquial expression for the people I have in mind — he or she is a *kaputter Typ*. He or she is broken, tuned out, kaput, without meaning or function. The German word *kaputt* refers to a machine or a thing, not to an organic whole. In the world of the *kaputter Typ*, there is no sense of relatedness to other people. Relationships are disturbed or even nonexistent. The language of the broken one cannot reach another person. She is unable to express her feelings, and her perception of the world is absurdly reduced. Her action does not make use of her capacities. The broken person has no trust in creation, no sense of her createdness or the possibility of empowerment. The broken person has been socialized in a culture that threatens all the capacities of human beings to take in creation in wonder and in awe, in self-renewal and in appreciation of beauty, in joy and in expressions of gratefulness and praise. Who then is the *kaputter Typ?* I will not answer this question, because we know him too well. You know him as I know her. After a long talk with a depressed student, I, exhausted from listening to him, finally asked, "Was there anything in the last year about which you felt some joy?" His response was that even the word "joy" had not come to his lips for two years, and he added that, objectively speaking, he had no use for such a word. He had never learned how to wonder or to be amazed.

Philosophy began with wondering, *thaumazein.* Wondering is part of our day-to-day experience as well. I recall when my youngest daughter learned to tell time. One day, in utter joy, she exclaimed, "Look, Mom, this is a truly wonderful five before half past six!" Perhaps children are the greatest conveyors of amazement. They do not bypass anything as too trivial or mundane. They free us from our banal and dull perspectives. To affirm creation means to enter into the freedom of amazement and delight. Nothing is simply available, usable, or to be taken for granted. The broken person will counter, "What is so special about it? It has always been that way." His capacity to trivialize everything has surpassed his capacity to wonder. He is crippled by a "dryness of the heart," as the mystics termed it. He no longer wonders about the wonders of the world. Children and artists are teachers of a spirituality of creation. They recombine created things into a new synthesis, and they change triviality into wonder, givenness into createdness. Through them we un-learn triviality and learn amazement; we again see the magnolia tree, and we see it as if for the first time.

Another element essential to a spirituality of creation is the human capacity to perceive beauty. We are able to notice, to ob-serve, to perceive in a purposeless way that we call aesthetics. In German, the verb "to perceive" is *wahrnehmen*. Its literal mean-ing, which is "to take something as true," demonstrates that perception is related to truth. Our aesthetic perception lures us into truth. When "the doors to perception are cleansed," as Blake put it, we see more and we perceive the created world in a different way. The world appears no longer as disposable dead stuff but as a vital growing organism. In aesthetics we are all animists who believe that there is a soul in every living be-ing. Our perception of aesthetic objects makes them responsive. A dialogue ensues between the perceiver and the otherwise in-animate object. We grasp the interrelatedness of creation in this dialogue between the sun and me, the birch and me. Perhaps then we see as God saw in the beginning when she said, "It is very good." The Hebrew word for good, *tov,* also means fair or beautiful. Thus God said on creating the universe, "Behold, it is all very beautiful." To love creation means to perceive its beauty in the most unexpected places. An aesthetic education that deepens our perception is not a luxury for the elite but a cultural necessity for everyone. To believe in creation is to per-ceive and to engage in the aesthetic mode of perception. One cannot love God if one does not know what beauty is:

> Ernesto Cardenal,
> questioned on how he came to be a poet, a priest,
> and a revolutionary,
> gave as his first reason
> love of beauty.

This led him, he said,
to poetry
(and beyond);
it led him to god
(and beyond);
it led him to the gospel
(and beyond);
it led him
to socialism
(and beyond).

How weak a love of beauty must be
that is content with house beautiful;
how trivial a love of poetry
that stops with the text;
how small a love of god
that becomes sated in him
not hungrier;
how little we love the gospel
if we keep it to ourselves;
how powerless are socialistic yearnings
if they fear
to go beyond what will be.

The most terrifying quality about the life of the broken person — both the one I meet and the one I am — is the absence
of joy. In the Jewish tradition, joy was understood as the most
natural response to our having been created, while sadness was
deemed a rejection of the gift of life. In this metaphysical sense,
joy is not derived from special events or the presents we receive;
it involves the mere delight in being alive and gratefulness for
the gift of life. But for an increasing number of people in secular
culture the expression "a gift of life" does not make too much
sense: If the giver disappears, why should we see life as a gift

at all, why should we not understand it instead as a biological accident, a casual event, an unforeseen occurrence that neither has nor requires an explanation? When life has lost its quality of being something given to us, it turns into a mere matter of fact. People grow up in this culture without any education for joy. Does the deep, reasonless joy of being alive die in a world without religion? Does it make a difference with regard to our capacity for enjoyment whether we live in a world we think is made by human beings or in one we believe to be created by God? I do not know the answer to these questions, yet I observe a remarkable absence of joy in secular, industrialized cultures. At the same time, my own spiritual experience teaches me that to recall creation, to be reminded of our createdness in a community of people who struggle together, enhances my own awareness of joy — of how much I need it, how much I yearn for it. A spirituality of creation reminds us that we were born for joy.

These elements of a creation-centered spirituality — wonder, renewal, a sense of beauty, and the capacity to rejoice — are integrated into the act of praising creation. To love someone is, among other things, to praise the person we love. To laud is another purposeless action of which only the human being is capable, at least consciously. The early church fathers said that even animals laud God, but without awareness. If we are in love with someone, we are seized by the need to make our love explicit, to speak about the beloved one. We rush to discover a language in which we can praise the beloved. Could it be that we are in love with creation, as God is according to James Weldon Johnson's poem? If this is true, then it is not enough to think about nature's beauty; we have to articulate it. Our feelings become stronger and clearer when we express them. We become better lovers of the earth when we tell the earth how beautiful it is. It takes time to learn how to praise the beauty of creation. On the way, we rekindle our gratitude and shed the self who took creation for granted. We recover the sense of awe before life; we recover the lost reverence and passion for the living. This is not a saccharine, superficial form of spirituality....

In her novel *The Color Purple,* Alice Walker presents a conversation between two black women about God, which is one of the best texts on religion in contemporary literature that I know of. The exchange between Celie and Shug has a dual thrust. On the one hand, it is a critique of traditional religion, its God-talk and its God-image; on the other hand, it is an attempt to affirm God in a new manner.

Celie has lived her life with a God-image that she now recognizes is dubious in the extreme. When Shug asks what Celie's God looks like, she sheepishly replies, "He big and old and tall and graybearded and white. He wear white robes and go barefooted." His eyes are "sort of bluish-gray. Cool. Big though. White lashes...." This God represents the power that white people have over blacks and that men have over women. With the awareness that the God she has been praying to all her life is a white man comes the shocking realization that she detests, and no longer needs, this God who "sit up there glorying in being deef...." Just as "white people never listen to colored, period," so this God has never listened to the cries of the black woman Celie, whose father was lynched, whose mother was deranged, whose stepfather raped her repeatedly, whose life, prior to meeting Shug, was stunted by unrelenting toil and humiliation. And yet Celie struggles with God. Her need for God persists past her burgeoning rejection of an outworn white male deity: "But deep in my heart I care about God. What he going to think. And come to find out, he don't think.... But it ain't easy, trying to do without God."

Shug has already laid to rest her once negative and empty concept of God: "When I found out I thought God was white, and a man, I lost interest." This realization, however, signaled the beginning of her religious journey, not the end. Inspired to move beyond "the old white man," Shug now challenges Celie with a full-blown conception of God that departs radically from white, patriarchal definitions:

> Here's the thing...the thing I believe. God is inside you and inside everybody else. You come into the world with God. But only them that search for it inside find it. And sometimes it just manifest itself even if you not looking, or don't know what you looking for. Trouble do it for most folks, I think. Sorrow, lord. Feeling like shit.

Hers is a creational spirituality. The dialogue between this God and Shug, who refers to God as "It" because "God ain't a he or a she," flows out of her awareness that everything in creation is of God. "Listen," she says to Celie, "God love everything you love — and a mess of stuff you don't." Shug's God-talk is grounded in her experience as a woman and in her love of life.

Shug's exceptional reflections on the relationship between God and humans climax in a passionate affirmation of the source of all life: "But more than anything else, God love admiration....I think it pisses God off if you walk by the color purple in a field somewhere and don't notice it." God is not synonymous with omnipotent control; rather, God's power lies in sharing life with others. The admiration God loves is our sense of connectedness with the whole of creation. We all have difficulties with praising the God of creation. We all often walk by the color purple in a field and don't notice it. But God does not give up trying to lure us into oneness with all creation.

—TWTL, 46–52

2

A Different Journey
Suffering and Resistance

The results of Soelle's mystical vision of religious experience are the focus of the second series of writings selected. The "different journey" is a sense of Soelle's contemporary look at mysticism which sees the spiritual journey as a via transformativa — a way of transformation. While traditionally "union" has been the goal of a mystical journey, and has often focused on ways that one is separated from the world in union with God, Soelle's mystical vision recognizes that becoming one with God does not mean being absorbed into a God-separate-from-the-world. Instead, union is about cooperation, interaction, standing together with God and others against the values of our culture, against the hold that ego, power, and violence have on us. To become one with God is to become one with God's purposes; to become one with creation is to recognize the value of all creation; to seek union is to resist the distorted values of our own culture and society. Thus the ultimate goal of mystical religious experience is resistance. For persons living in the first world, Soelle's main audience, resistance to the status quo in the form of social and political praxis is the call of God. While liberation is the most appropriate image for those who live on the

margins and in situations of great oppression, the spiritual jour-
ney of those in positions of power and privilege in society is a
journey of resistance to the very situations and values that pro-
vided such privilege in the first place. We are empowered by
God to act in the world, not to meet the suffering of others
with indifference. We are called not to anesthetize ourselves to
the suffering in our own lives or in the lives of others, but to
stand with the victims of our world, to eliminate suffering when
we are able, and to find meaning in suffering that cannot be al-
leviated. Our actions are God's actions; our hands are God's
hands. When we see with God's eyes we are compelled to stand
against whatever opposes the reign of God in the world. For
Soelle one form of such resistance was her political activism
in the peace movement, where she stood against nuclear arms,
the Vietnam War, and injustice in Latin America. But it also
occurred in her writings, from theological treatises to prayer,
which called for a different type of spiritual journey.

GOD ON THE GALLOWS

How can hope be expressed in the face of senseless suffering?

I begin with a story that Elie Wiesel, a survivor of Auschwitz, relates in his book *Night*:

> The SS hung two Jewish men and a boy before the assem-
> bled inhabitants of the camp. The men died quickly but
> the death struggle of the boy lasted half an hour. "Where
> is God? Where is he?" a man behind me asked. As the boy,
> after a long time, was still in agony on the rope, I heard
> the man cry again, "Where is God now?" And I heard a
> voice within me answer, "Here he is — he is hanging here
> on this gallows.... "

It is difficult to speak about this experience. One has not yet traveled the way that leads from the question to the answer simply by reflecting on it theologically. The reflection stands in danger of missing the way itself since it is bound to other situations and thus cannot comprehend the question.

Within Jewish religious thinking the answer given here is understood in terms of the shekinah, the "indwelling presence of God in the world." According to cabalistic teaching God does not forsake the suffering world, in need of redemption after the fall. "His glory itself descends to the world, enters into it, into 'exile,' dwells in it, dwells with the troubled, the suffering creatures in the midst of their uncleanness — desiring to redeem them." In his emptied, abased form God shares the suffering of his people in exile, in prison, in martyrdom. Wandering, straying, dispersed, his indwelling rests in things and awaits the redemption of God through his creatures. God suffers where people suffer. God must be delivered from pain. "It is not merely in appearance that God has entered into exile in His indwelling in the world; it is not merely in appearance that in His indwelling He suffers with the fate of His world." So one can say that God, in the form of this shekinah, hangs on the gallows at Auschwitz and waits "for the initial movement toward redemption to come from the world..." (Buber). Redemption does not come to people from outside or from above. God wants to use people in order to work on the completion of his creation. Precisely for this reason God must also suffer with the creation.

To interpret this story within the framework of the Christian tradition, it is Christ who suffers and dies here. To be sure, one must ask the effect of such an interpretation, which connects Christ with those gassed in Auschwitz and those burned with napalm in Vietnam. Wherever one compares the incomparable — for instance, the Romans' judicial murder of a first-century religious leader and the fascist genocide in the twentieth century — there, in a sublime manner, the issue is robbed of clarity, indeed the modern horror is justified. The point of view from which the comparison proceeds is not the number of victims nor the method of killing. A fifty-year-old woman piece worker hangs on the cross no less than Jesus — only longer. The only thing that can be compared is the person's relationship to the suffering laid upon him, his learning, his change. The justification for a Christian interpretation can only be established when it undergirds and clarifies what the story from Auschwitz contains.

In Jesus' passion history a decisive change occurs, the change from the prayer to be spared to the dreadfully clear awareness that that would not happen. The way from Gethsemane to Golgotha is a taking leave of (narcissistic) hope. It is the same change that occurs in the story from Auschwitz: the eye is directed away from the almighty Father to the sufferer himself. But not in such a way that this sufferer now has to endure everything alone. The essence of Jesus' passion history is the assertion that this one whom God forsook himself becomes God. Jesus does not die like a child who keeps waiting for his father. His "Eli, Eli" is a scream of growing up, the pain of this cry is a birth pang. When religion, which one can comprehend as the bundle of defense mechanisms against disappointment, intensifies one's holding fast to his father, then "faith [accomplishes] part of the task Freud assigns to whoever undertakes to 'do without his father...'" (Ricoeur).

The task of doing without one's father is accomplished in the story transmitted from Auschwitz, though to be sure in a way different from that in the mythical story of the death and resurrection of Christ. The mythical story is separated here, divided among individual voices. What Jesus experienced in himself is here assigned to three different characters. The man behind the

narrator cries what Jesus cried; the boy died, as did Jesus; and
the narrator hears a voice that tells him where God is, rather,
who God is — the victim. But while Jesus is the question, victim, and answer in one person, in this story all communication
breaks down. The questioner does not get the answer; the message does not reach the dying one, and the narrator remains
alone with his voice, a fact one can scarcely endure.

The decisive phrase, that God is hanging "here on this gallows," has two meanings. First, it is an assertion about God.
God is no executioner — and no almighty spectator (which
would amount to the same thing). God is not the mighty tyrant.
Between the sufferer and the one who causes the suffering, between the victim and the executioner, God, whatever people
make of this word, is on the side of the sufferer. God is on the
side of the victim, he is hanged.

Second, it is an assertion about the boy. If it is not also an assertion about the boy, then the story is false and one can forget
about the first assertion. But how can the assertion about the
boy be made without cynicism? "He is with God, he has been
raised, he is in heaven." Such traditional phrases are almost always clerical cynicism with a high apathy content. Sometimes
one stammers such phrases which are in fact true as a child repeats something he doesn't understand, with confidence in the
speaker and the language that has still not become part of him.
That is always possible, but in the long run it destroys those
who do it because learning to believe also means learning to
speak, and it is theologically necessary to transcend the shells
of our inherited language. What language can possibly serve
not only to preserve for all the life asserted by classical theology but primarily to translate it into a language of liberation?
We would have to learn to hear the confession of the Roman
centurion, "Truly this was God's son," in the phrase, "Here he
is — he is hanging here on this gallows." Every single one of the

six million was God's beloved son. Were anything else the case, resurrection would not have occurred, even in Jesus' case.

God is not in heaven; he is hanging on the cross. Love is not an otherworldly, intruding, self-asserting power — and to meditate on the cross can mean to take leave of that dream.

Precisely those who in suffering experience the strength of the weak, who incorporate the suffering into their lives, for whom coming through free of suffering is no longer the highest goal, precisely they are there for the others who, with no choice in the matter, are crucified in lives of senseless suffering. A different salvation, as the language of metaphysics could promise it, is no longer possible. The God who causes suffering is not to be justified even by lifting the suffering later. No heaven can rectify Auschwitz. But the God who is not a greater Pharaoh has justified himself: in sharing the suffering, in sharing the death on the cross.

God has no other hands than ours. Even "the future," which today is often supposed to translate the mythical word "heaven," cannot alter the fact that the boy had to die that way in Auschwitz.... But perhaps this future can preserve the memory of these children and thereby put up a better fight against death.

It is no less significant for us than it is for the boy that God is the one hanging on this gallows. God has no other hands than ours, which are able to act on behalf of other children.

The objection can be raised that even with this thought the dead are still "being used" for the living. They are to help us, to change us. That is perhaps true — but is any other relationship with the dead conceivable? Doesn't all remembering of them and all praying for them, all eating in remembrance of them have this character, that we "need" the dead in a double sense, of wanting them and of making use of them? They have been taken from us and are unable to prevent this use of themselves. But there is no way for us to love them other than to incorporate them into our work at living. There is no other way but to consume them — and perhaps that represents a debt we owed them that cannot be paid in life. Through our behavior we can turn them into "the devil's martyrs" posthumously, who confirm the eternal cycle of injustice under the sun and bring ourselves to speechlessness; or we can use them for praise to God.

In this sense those who suffer in vain and without respect depend on those who suffer in accord with justice. If there were no one who said, "I die, but I shall live," no one who said, "I and the Father are one," then there would be no hope for those who suffer mute and devoid of hoping. All suffering would then be senseless, destructive pain that could not be worked on, all grief would be "worldly grief" and would lead to death. But we know of people who have lived differently, suffered differently. There is a history of resurrections, which has vicarious significance. A person's resurrection is no personal privilege for himself alone — even if he is called Jesus of Nazareth. It contains within itself hope for all, for everything.

— SU, 145–50

ONENESS OF JOY AND SUFFERING

The mystical experience of God, which always includes the possibility of missing God, arises from the concrete situation and necessarily returns to it: transforming, acting, suffering. A spirituality that unfolds apart from real history and seeks to be left alone by it may match certain features of piety. But this is not "mystical" in the sense developed here when it shuns

the cost of God's presence in the world's activity and its suffering. The "dark night of the soul" does not fall outside the
historical world in an allegedly pure encounter of God and the
individual soul. At least in the tradition we call Judeo-Christian,
that encounter is always marked by the irksome and irrevocable
presence of the other whom the Hebrew Bible called "the neighbor." The "dark night" that can purify perception and spirit so
that they may be guided from the onset of darkness, to mid-
night, and on to dawn, is always a night the place of which
can be named. The "dark night of the soul" experienced today
is based in a "dark night of the world." Its eclipse of God is
given expression in a variety of accents or with different names
of hopelessness, such as "cross" (Edith Stein), "misfortune"
(Simone Weil), and "agony" (Reinhold Schneider).

I begin with the dark night of the Jewish people and, at
the same time, of the worlds of those twelve years of German history about the horrors of which, according to Reinhold
Schneider, "no insightful person can assert that it is impossible
to repeat them." A Roman Catholic woman and mystic of Jewish birth gave that night the traditional name "cross." Edith
Stein (1891–1942), a philosopher and Edmund Husserl's assis-
tant, was first an atheist and subsequently a Carmelite sister.
She wrote a study on John of the Cross in 1941 titled *Kreuzes-
wissenschaft* (Science of the cross). "A *scientia crucis* can be had
only when one comes to experience the cross most profoundly.
I was persuaded of this from the very beginning and said with a
full heart: *Ave Crux, spes unica!* (Hail, Cross, unique hope!)."
Born into an educated, Jewish, merchant family, from early on
and without much ado she called herself an atheist. What oriented the way of an intellectually gifted phenomenologist to
mysticism was, above all, her experience of suffering. One of
her closest philosophical friends from the time of her studies in

Göttingen was killed in 1917 at the front in Flanders. His partner, Ann Reinach, who during the First World War converted
from Judaism to Christianity, responded to that senseless death
quite differently than Edith Stein had expected. In the midst of
pain she accepted her suffering in light of the cross, without
regarding it as a pointless blow of fate, or sinking into deaden-
ing dullness or self-destructiveness. She saw it as her personal
participation in the cross.

Edith Stein said that this encounter was "the moment when
my disbelief broke down and Christ shone forth, Christ in the
mystery of the cross." Years later, when she was received into
the Carmelite community, she confessed that "it is not human
action that can help us but Christ's suffering. To take part in
it is what I desire." In 1933, at age forty-two, Edith Stein entered the Carmelite community at Cologne, a step that deeply
pained her religious Jewish mother. All attempts of her sisters
and brothers to stop her failed, including their offer to support her financially when, in April 1933, she lost her job for
reasons of her Jewishness. A twelve-year-old niece asked her at
the time why she was doing this now. Her niece later wrote,
"By becoming Roman Catholic, our aunt forsook her people.
Her entry into the monastery gave witness to the world outside
that she wanted to separate herself from the Jewish people."
That is how it appeared to her family, but it was never true for
Edith Stein herself. She did not cut herself off but went with
her people on their way, albeit in the perspective of theology of
the cross that to the majority of Jewish persons could only be
incomprehensible, if not unbearable.

Reflecting on the mysticism of suffering and its biggest
symbol, the Roman Empire's instrument of torture, must by necessity confront traditional Christian anti-Judaism. Edith Stein
was not immune to it even though she rejected the absurd notion of the collective guilt of Jews for the death of Jesus. She

deeply desired that all Jews would convert, and she suffered much from the rejection on the part of the Jews of the Messiah promised to and longed for precisely by them. In her last will and testament, composed on June 9, 1939, she wrote: "I pray to the Lord that he may accept my living and my dying...as an atonement for the Jewish people's unbelief and so that the Lord may be accepted by his own and that his reign may come in glory, that Germany may be saved and that there be peace in the world." Burdened with the false judgment concerning this alleged unbelief, which has become more apparent even for Christians since Auschwitz, Edith Stein lived in solidarity with the Jewish people as a conscientious Christian. In 1942, when the SS took her away to the transports headed for Auschwitz, she said to her cloister sisters, "Pray for me!" She took her biological sister Rosa, who was mentally disabled, and went with her into the gas chamber. She took Rosa by the hand with these words, "Come, we go for our people."

Edith Stein understood the fate of the Jewish people as "participation in the cross of Christ." It is not a dolorousness that seeks suffering and then chooses which one to shoulder; rather, it is a mystical approach to the reality that comes from the passive experience of being overwhelmed to accept voluntarily the suffering of the downcast and insulted. In Roman Catholicism, such acceptance is often called "sacrifice," which is in my judgment an insufficient term. In what others call "fate," acceptance finds the suffering God and calls her/him "Love," and thus the accepting person becomes a participating subject instead of remaining a mere object of the power of fate. Acceptance deprives icy meaninglessness of its power because it clings to God's warmth also in suffering. In this context, sacrifice does not mean that a God hostile to life and humans has to be placated with blood, or that a saving quality accrues to suffering as such. Rather, that concept expresses the participation of humans who do not acquiesce but who, in mystical defiance, insist through their suffering that nothing become lost. It is in this sense that in 1930, twelve years before her death in Auschwitz, Edith Stein spoke of the *holocaustum,* what the Bible calls the complete sacrifice, when she thought about her attempts to reach half-hearted or unbelieving people with her words. "After every meeting in which the impossibility of influencing someone is palpably present to me, the urgency of my own *holocaustum* becomes even more intense." And, at the end of 1938, when several of her siblings had already emigrated from Germany — all others were subsequently murdered by the Nazis — she reflected on the name she took as a nun, Theresa Benedicta of the Holy Cross: "To me the cross means the fate of God's people that was beginning to make itself felt even then. I thought that they who understood that it was the cross of Christ would take it upon themselves in the name of all."

To think of Auschwitz as a continuation of Golgotha is horrendous for a Jewish mind. I became personally aware of this during a conversation with Wanda Kampmann, a historian, whose book *Deutsche und Juden* (Germans and Jews) appeared in 1963. I said at the time that Christ had been gassed in Auschwitz; she could not stand that way of speaking. I was startled and felt ashamed, for I really believed — and still do — that Christ cannot be understood and loved without seeing the ongoing crucifixion done to his sisters and brothers. On the other hand, I had the feeling that in uttering it I was betraying this truth. Today I understand better the dread of a Christian co-optation of an event that needs its own language, the Jewish language, and that has found it in many forms. I will not cease to question critically the silence of dominant Christian theology that does not wish to see Christ's ongoing suffering in the Shoah. In that sense, Edith Stein remains a mystical-theological teacher of "what it means to be betrothed to the Lord in the sign of the cross. Admittedly, one will never comprehend it because it is a mystery."

The craziness of Edith Stein may well be compared to that of the French woman Simone Weil and perhaps be expressed in Reinhold Schneider's pointed formulation that identifies agony (*Agonie*) and numbness (*Narkose*) as the options open to us in the face of suffering. This expresses a basic conflict that applies to every mysticism of suffering of the past and present century. The conflict consists of the contradiction between the avoidance of suffering, not-having-seen and not-wanting-to-see anything, and seeking to protect oneself with the diverse and increasingly improving means of numbing, on the one hand; and the preferential option for victims wherein people voluntarily enter into the pain of others and, in the extreme case, choose the pain of death, on the other. "Numbness" is a metaphor for apathy, "agony" one for compassion.

Simone Weil, too, chose agony before numbness. Rarely did a modern intellectual human being so passionately, absurdly, pathologically resist every alleviation of pain, every social privilege, and every right to numbing as she did. It is said that when she was a child and was helping her parents move to another place, she found out that her burden was lighter than her brother's. She refused to walk any further until she was given a heavier load. In a certain sense, she did the same throughout her whole short life.

Like Edith Stein, she occupied herself intensively with the study of John of the Cross. Like him, she desired to overcome her natural dependency, especially on nourishment and healthcare but also the dependency on the reason that has to be subjected to faith, in favor of an inner emptiness that renders one open to God. Her concept for the dark night of the world is *malheur* (meaning not only unhappiness or sorrow, but affliction, a condition compounded of pain and distress).

It emerged for her in the context of the factory job that she held for one year while studying at the training college for secondary school teachers in Paris, interrupted by her medically unexplained excruciating migraine headaches. That self-chosen experiment, rooted in her trade union and socialist engagement, gave her a sense of what it means to live without dignity and rights.

On June 26, 1935, while on a bus, she recorded in her factory diary certain feelings that were to become everyday reality for Jews in Germany. "How can a slave like me get on this bus and use it just like everyone else for a payment of twelve centimes? What uncommon advantage! Were I told to get off because such convenient means of transportation were not there for me to use and to go on foot instead, I believe that I would find that quite natural. Slavery has utterly deprived me of the feeling that I have any rights. It seems like sheer grace to experience moments when I do not have to experience human brutality." *Malheur* (a totalization of suffering) causes people to become deadened and to give up on themselves as well as to be unable to resist or accept suffering. During her time at the factory, "the affliction (*malheur*) of others penetrated [my very] flesh and soul. . . . The mark of slavery was stamped on me forever, like that mark of shame that the Romans branded with a hot iron on the foreheads of their most despised slaves. Ever since, I have regarded myself as a slave."

The manifold attempts of self-sacrifice in Simone Weil's life have to be understood from this radical perspective from below, from that of the victims of history. She worked like a Trojan in factory and farm. She took part in the Spanish Civil War on the side of the anti-Fascists. She advanced the idea of frontline nurses who would give aid at the very places of death, only to be ridiculed by Charles de Gaulle. She joined a parachute action in France so that she might fight in the underground. In the end, she died as a consequence of eating only as much as was apportioned to Jews who had been left in France — a hunger ration she had imposed on herself as a token of her solidarity with them. "When you, steadfastly clinging to love, sink to the point where you can no longer suppress the cry, 'My God, why have you forsaken me?' but then hold out there without ceasing to suffer, you will finally touch something that is no longer affliction (*malheur*) and not joy either, but the pure, supra-sensual, most inward essential being common to both joy and suffering." Simone Weil did indeed despise numbness; in agony she cried out to God rather than do without such cries. She did not regard Christianity as a "supernatural remedy for suffering"; miracles or punishments or interventions of supernatural power have no place whatsoever in her thinking. She insisted that Christianity's greatness lies in that it seeks what she called a supernatural use for suffering. In her work, as in the book of Job, *malheur* (this "inconsolable bitterness") and the love of God are juxtaposed, but that is something that she is not conscious of, given her inherited Christian anti-Judaism.

This mystically experienced oneness of joy and suffering shines forth from the agony present in many experiences of suffering free of numbness. It is an inconsolability that stays steadfastly in the love for God. "To love God, beyond the destruction of Troy and Carthage and without consolation. Love is not consolation. It is light."   — SC, 146–51

GOD IN THE FLESH

A Christian understanding of the incarnation contradicts any purely idealist interpretation of it. For incarnation means that God has entered precisely into sensuous and social reality and that therefore he cannot be experienced apart from corporeality and society.

Many religions and quasi-religious worldviews promise their followers an experience of God in other media and other realms of existence: in nature, in timeless eternity, or in the depths of the human soul. These various possible ways of forging a link with the totality of things and of achieving meaning are real and can be documented in the history of religions. But in contrast to all these possible ways, the Judeo-Christian tradition has taken another path, one that leads through history. It experiences meaning and happiness in history, and historical events are the ones it celebrates, interprets, and repeats. The events by which it lives can be dated: the Exodus of the Jewish people from Egyptian slavery, the resurrection of Jesus from the dead. By "historical experiences" I mean here experiences having to do with the body and society. They have a physical, public relevance. Despite widespread tendencies to spiritualization, this basic materialist thrust of Christianity can be neither denied nor eliminated. A certain fidelity to the earth and to the real experiences of its inhabitants caused the development of certain hopes that appeal to the biblical tradition.

According to the classical view, Christ is God in the conditions of human existence. He renounced the divine attributes that transcend human existence; he stripped himself of them. He willed not to be omniscient, omnipotent, and omnipresent; he plunged fully into the conditions set by the world: he became a slave in a slaveholding society, he experienced hunger and thirst, cold and pain, like all the others who did not have the wealth that would have protected them from such experiences.

The cross is the climactic and clearest symbol of this unique occurrence in the history of religions. It was an instrument of class struggle, wielded from above and used to discipline rebels — that is, runaway slaves and tenants who fled the land

and could not pay their debts. It was an atrocious instrument
of torture that stripped death of any dignity and reduced sacrifice to torment. We understand the cross only if we have a
material understanding of what it meant in physical and social
terms. "Were you there when they nailed him to the tree?" asks
the spiritual, the religious song of black slaves. Those who sang
it had to reckon with the real possibility of being lynched, of
hanging on a tree as its alien fruit. "Were you there when they
crucified my Lord?" they sang, in order to achieve self-identity
and see their own lives mirrored in the old story. "Were you
there when the sun refused to shine?" Christianity is a religion
of slaves and does not need Nietzsche's exhortation about being
faithful to the earth, because its God is not to be found except
in the flesh.   — "Between," 90–91

THE CROSS

The cross expresses the bitter, realistic depth of faith and is a
symbol of this-worldliness and history. It was not theologians
who invented the cross, rather, the Roman Empire thought up
this method of deterring people who heard the cry for liberation by slowly and publicly torturing to death those who cried
out. Anyone who has ever read reports of torture, for example
from Guatemala, anyone who has seen a film like *Two Worlds*
about South Africa knows that it is not a matter of something
exotic but of the normality of imperial suppression which now
presents a slow method of torture as "low intensity conflict"
for whole regions.

It was not God who erected the cross but the lords of this
world, whether they are named Pharaoh or Somoza, Pilate or
Botha. To go in search of a soft God seems to me like an attempt to emigrate to a distant South Sea island, as if there were

no nuclear weapons tests there and no grooming of women for the prostitution trade. The soft God has long been here; I cannot imagine him any softer than our brother from Nazareth. But the actual problem that we have with Jesus and the cross is our wish to get away, to hide with the Father.

It is not God who makes us suffer. But love has its price. God wants to make us alive, and the wider we open our hearts to others or the more audibly we cry out against the injustice which rules over us, the more difficult our life in the rich society of injustice becomes. Even a small love of a few trees, of seals, or of schoolchildren who cry out at night in torment from lowflying aircraft is costly. Many cannot afford even a small love for creatures and prefer not to have seen anything.

And yet there is still today this opposite experience of many Christian men and women: these persons treat themselves to kindness and permit themselves the bit of justice and care for others without which we cannot become human.

There are among us people who allow themselves the truth. They step in for the victims of violence; they create unrest while the authorities are trying to keep everything nicely under control. There is great inner freedom in choosing life even when this choice plunges us into difficulties, unpleasantness, indeed suffering.

I would like to say something in praise of this freedom because I believe that we misunderstand the cross when we make it into a necrophilic, death-seeking symbol. We not only get ill at the cross, we are free to avoid the cross in the apartheid of the middle class or to take it upon ourselves with all the difficulties we enter into when we get seriously involved.

Jesus too was free to go as far as the cross: he could have remained peacefully in Galilee; his friends urged him to avoid the cross. Women whom I know in Nicaragua could have gone to Miami or let themselves be recruited by the C.I.A. No one forced them to remain with the revolution. Members of their families, mostly men, did in fact take the road to the golf courses of Miami. But the women stayed and tried to do the will of God; this original act of freedom has its price. For them the cross is a symbol of the love of life in justice. It expresses love for the endangered, threatened life of God in our world.

The more you grow into love, into the message of Jesus — to say it in such traditional, defenseless terms — the more vulnerable you make yourself. You simply become more open to attack when you have become conspicuous or when "that of God" lights up in you. When you spread your life around rather than hoarding it, then the great light becomes visible within you. To be sure, you enter into loneliness, often you lose friends, a standard of living, a job, or a secure career, but at the same time you are changed. And the cross, this sign of isolation, of shame, of abandonment becomes, in this process, the tree of life, which you no longer like to be without at all. The dead wood of martyrdom begins to turn green. And you know at once where you belong.

To choose life means to embrace the cross. It means to put up with the cross, the difficulties, the lack of success, the fear of standing alone. Tradition has never promised us a rose garden. To embrace the cross today means to grow into resistance. And the cross will turn green and blossom. We survive the cross. We grow in suffering. We are the tree of life.   —TS, 102–4

LOVING THE CROSS

A compromise between the stoic and Christian-mystical concepts of suffering is actually impossible. One needs to compare the artistic portrayals in Roman portraits with those out of the autumn of the Middle Ages in order to see the difference between stoic self-restricting tranquility and the "sweetness" of mystical suffering. One needs to compare the prosaic language of the consolatories from the Middle Ages, with their classification of various benefits and advantages that can attract the soul out of suffering, with the erotically tinted language of mystical texts in order to recognize the incompatibility of these two ways of arranging and conquering suffering. Of course, within Western history there were attempts again and again to combine a stoic and a Christian interpretation, baroque tragedy offering perhaps the most significant example. But the starting and finishing points still remain incompatible. The stoic denies suffering and by a gesture of tranquility does not allow it to enter his soul. The consolatories of the Middle Ages are stoic and ascetic in orientation. Their ideal is the *senex sapiens,* "the wise old man," not the mystics' lover of God. With a prosaic matter-of-factness and harshness their instructions on how to overcome suffering present, on the one hand, possibilities for the avoidance of suffering and, on the other, use of unavoidable suffering. Stoicism in the Middle Ages is aware that a person's true happiness lies exclusively within, independent of outer circumstances and of Fortuna, the ancient goddess of joy, by now often viewed sarcastically and pessimistically. From Fortuna, from entrusting oneself to her care, comes suffering; only by training oneself to achieve tranquility can a person secure a place to stand in the face of such suffering. What people call evil is only illusionary and does not touch the wise.

This spiritual line continues in the Renaissance and forms a "closed type of suffering theory," which inevitably stresses the ancient concept of fate. The alternation of the rhythm of life entails suffering as something natural. The supernatural, that is, the understanding of suffering as something that produces change, recedes.

While in the language of mysticism "calmness" designates the frame of mind of a person who has renounced himself and all things and become free for God, the meaning of the word later shifts to the stoic concept of suffering: the source of calmness is no longer God but indifference; the absence of emotions brings people to a world-conquering coldness, which moves along with a tone of resignation.

The exterior and distorted form of this stance is apathy, which is incapable of suffering. The attempt to keep suffering from entering the soul is indeed only possible if it is a limited, for example, physical, suffering which has not reached the three-dimensionality of which Simone Weil speaks. The night of being abandoned by God is not experienced in this case; it is impossible to be forsaken by the God *Logos* (Reason).

A significant representative of this viewpoint in this century is the late Bertolt Brecht. The suggestions he gives for dealing with suffering caused by political power all amount to making oneself small, untouchable, insensitive; only he who keeps everything at arm's length will survive. The ancient stoic advice to live in seclusion lingers on here. Tranquility unites with indifference and cunning at the same time. It saves itself for the day that is coming after the dark times of power. Freud also approaches the stoic line in his understanding of suffering that cannot be averted. One can view his criticism of religion as a criticism of people's false and excessive expectations and desires. "Our God, Logos, will fulfill whichever of these wishes nature outside us allows.... He promises no compensation for us, who suffer grievously from life" (Freud). In contrast to the "illusion" which religion represents, *Logos* and *Ananke* (Necessity) designate the true God. The acknowledgment of this God brings with it the endurance of suffering, which is seen as a necessary part of life.

Socially and politically expressed, tranquility is an ideal for the upper classes, just as the apathetic God is not the God of the little people and their pain. In stoic piety the present world and humanity within it are seen as good; indeed the world is seen as "Zeus's perfect city," so that any revolt must appear unthinkable, indeed absurd.

The Christian understanding of suffering, as it expresses itself in the mysticism of the cross, is different from this. Here the stance over against suffering is not that of averting or avoiding it. For the religion of slaves and of the poor, avoidance and "the hidden life" are not real possibilities. The mystical way points in the opposite direction: the soul is open to suffering, abandons itself to suffering, holds back nothing. It does not make itself small and untouchable, distant and insensitive; it is affected by suffering in the fullest possible way. The extreme and distorted form of this stance is masochism. Its distortion consists in anticipating the pleasure that deliverance affords; the way is mistaken for the goal. But a true acceptance of suffering is never a self-sufficiency which would be at peace and satisfied already now in the devil's inn. The acceptance of suffering by giving oneself over to it rather than facing it with tranquility arises out of a different relationship to the future. The God who says, "Behold, I make all things new" (Rev. 21:5), cannot himself exist now without suffering over what is old. What is promised is not only a restoration of elemental goodness after the storm of power, but the abolition of all power by which some men dominate others, all anguish. That is why, in the Christian understanding of suffering, mysticism and revolution move so close to one another.

"For God only speaks in his creatures' proneness to suffering, which the hearts of unbelievers don't possess" (Müntzer). This "proneness to suffering," that is, the suffering that a person has experienced as well as the capacity to suffer, is what makes him stronger than anything that comes his way. What is meant is not only that it is better to suffer wrong than to do it, although this thought — with its rejection of the illusion of neutrality — does play a role in the Christian explanation of suffering. But what is decisive for Christian mysticism is first of all the knowledge that the one who suffers wrong is also stronger (not just morally better) than the one who does wrong. That "God is always with the one who is suffering" entails not only consolation but also strengthening: a rejection of every ideology of punishment, which was so useful for the cementing of privileges and for oppression. There is a mystical defiance that rebels against everything ordained and regulated from on high and holds fast to the truth it has discovered. "Not God himself, not angels, nor any sort of creature is able to separate from God the soul who is in the image of God" (Eckhart). That is the extension of Paul's thought: Nothing "can separate us from the love of God" (Rom. 8:39).

The Christian idea of the acceptance of suffering means something more than and different from what is expressed in the words "put up with, tolerate, bear." With these words the object, the suffering itself, remains unchanged. It is borne — as a burden, suffered — as an injustice; it is tolerated, although intolerable; borne, although unbearable. "Put up with" and "tolerate" point to stoic tranquility rather than to Christian acceptance. The word "take," also in its combination with "on, up, over," means that the person doing the accepting is himself changed. What I "take" belongs to me in a different sense from something I only bear. I receive a guest, agree to a proposal, take on an assignment; I say yes, I consent, I assent, I agree with.

This stance of acceptance is suspect in a two-fold way. With respect to the individual it can be taken as masochism, with respect to society as affirmation. It is "affirmative," serving to stabilize existing conditions; it is seen as a false reconciliation, a naive identification with that which "is," though it is in no sense very good. Isn't it only veiled submission, with all the social consequences that have attended Christianity's cult of suffering? For centuries this cult of suffering has been shamelessly exploited to justify injustice and oppression. Acceptance of suffering is an essential element in "piety," to use a key word for what is contained in the traditional concept of religion: "the pious attachment to the divine or the holy on the one side and on the other side its sociologically objective appearance" (Schlette). The tendency to accept existing social and political realities stems from this piety. It is, of course, evident that this period of piety has come to an end, at least in regard to the acceptance of suffering. In this sphere piety no longer means submission, but insurance against suffering at almost any cost. It shows an absence of piety to be uninsured, to have taken no preventive actions, to have made no provisions for defense or for a place to hide.

Both objections to a Christian acceptance of suffering, that of masochism and that of affirmation, apply more readily to past than to present practice. Society, now free of religion and tending toward apathy, is more at home with affirmation than the residue of religious culture is able to be. Gone is the old connection between accepting personally experienced suffering and affirming social conditions which make suffering necessary. Today affirmation of existing conditions is not forced through suffering, and it needs no religious basis. Today all suffering, especially suffering that is obvious and not hidden, is a contradiction to the prevailing fashion. If the voice of religion in earlier times repeated, "Bear it patiently," today affirmation arises in entirely different places, where people are told that perpetual happiness is readily available. That is done completely in the interest of this prevailing fashion. Only when sorrow is suppressed and hidden can this kind of affirmation be maintained.

That applies also to seemingly radical formulations that, in the garb of enlightenment, recommend "abolition" as the answer to suffering. Then the slogan in respect to suffering is not "acceptance but abolition," as if the questions that suffering raises — even a single one of them — could be answered in that way! It is a kind of submission theology in reverse, only now the Lord who has given and who has taken away is no longer called God but the future society, and it promises: the Lord who has given will not afterward take it away. Of course, it is necessary to relate every personal sorrow to society, that is, first to ask about its social causes, and then also to recognize that social conditions help determine the way in which suffering is endured and worked on. But that is not all that needs to be taken into account. If capitalism tries to make people believe that all affliction they encounter is their personal concern, their tough luck, to be endured by them, things are no different with a socialism that asserts the opposite. The concrete powerlessness then is left to those who today suffer wrongly in a distorted society. The expression "to abolish" takes suffering, which is an activity, an experience that people are involved in, and makes it a marketable commodity that one can acquire and get rid of.

Bazon Brock's provocative remark is to be understood in a similar way: "Death, that damned obscenity, must finally be abolished. Whoever speaks a word of comfort is a traitor." The substance of a thought of this kind is fascistic: death may no longer be interpreted, integrated, bemoaned, or surrounded by consolation. It must be removed from the realm of human experience. If it can be acquired, so it can also be abolished. And to accomplish this task of abolishing death, beyond the capacity of mere mortals, society looks to science. Then this god has the task of deciding who is worthy and unworthy of living.

Behind many of these considerations stand attempts to remove the problem of suffering from its global universality and to get a handle on it by dividing it in various possible ways. The most important of these distinctions is that between biologically derived and socially caused suffering. And these two categories are subdivided to distinguish between suffering that we can abolish and suffering we can at best soften. But as the case of the blinded Jacques Lusseyran clearly shows, the natural cause means virtually nothing compared with the social situation, on which the conquest even of natural and irreversible suffering decisively depends. Then all suffering would be dependent on the situation that people have created for one another and the share of purely natural suffering reduced to a minimum. That all suffering is social suffering, then, means that all suffering is to be worked on. No suffering can be clothed and transfigured any longer with the appearance of fate. But in that case it would also be unnecessary to rob natural suffering, precisely as purely natural, of its importance over against societal suffering that "can be abolished."

On the contrary, the help that a society gives to those who suffer from natural causes, for instance those who are incurably ill, is a measure of its humanity. The attempt at divisions becomes problematic when one believes he can distinguish "right" and "wrong" suffering. Certainly the suffering of the proletarian masses is objectively more important than that of a single artist. But this kind of "objectivity," applied consistently, destroys the capacity to perceive any suffering at all. Every unit can be relativized and minimized over against a greater whole. It is a macabre spectacle to draw up a balance sheet that ranks people's sufferings in order of importance.

We should not make it easy for ourselves and wish to distinguish between right and wrong suffering, between proletarian and middle-class suffering, between a child's affliction and that of a band of guerrillas, between that of an artist such as Kafka or Pavese and that of an insignificant salesgirl.

There is no wrong suffering. There is imaginary, sham, feigned, simulated, pretended suffering. But the assertion that someone suffers for the right or wrong reason presupposes a divine, all-penetrating judgment able to distinguish historically obsolete forms of suffering from those in our time, instead of leaving this decision to the sufferers themselves. Even the pain of children which can easily be alleviated is suffering that is neither right nor wrong. The division into meaningless and potentially meaningful suffering seems to me to come closest to reality. There is meaningless suffering on which people can no longer work, since it has destroyed all their essential powers.

Following an idea of Paul Tillich's, I would like to distinguish this meaningless suffering from suffering that can be meaningful since it impels one to act and thereby produces change. Christianity demands, says Tillich, "that one accept suffering with courage as an element of finitude and affirm finitude in spite of the suffering that accompanies it." It is clear that Christianity makes an overwhelming affirmation of suffering, far stronger than many other worldviews that do not have as their center the symbol of the cross. But this affirmation is only part of the great love for life as a whole that Christians express with the word "believe." To be able to believe means to say yes to this life, to this finitude, to work on it and hold it open for the promised future.

"Not to accept an event which happens in the world is to wish that the world did not exist." This statement of Simone Weil's sounds extreme, but it expresses with precision the sin of despair by which radical and unconditional affirmation of reality is destroyed. Suffering can bring us to the point of wishing that the world did not exist, of believing that nonbeing is better than being. It can make us despair and destroy our capacity for affirmation. We then cease loving God. "To wish that the world did not exist is to wish that I, just as I am, may be every-thing" (Weil). This wish is the state of sin. The person is curved in upon himself; pain has caused introversion. He has no future and can no longer love anything. He himself is everything; that is, he is dead. To be able to live we need affirmation:

> Almost all have called the world their friend
> Before they get their handful of earth in the end.
> (Brecht)

In this sense Christianity actually has an "affirmative" core; just as people who dare to bring a child into this world are act-ing "affirmatively." To put it in Christian terms, the affirmation of suffering is part of the great yes to life as a whole and not, as it sometimes can appear, the sole and the decisive affirma-tion, behind which the affirmation of life disappears entirely. The Bible speaks about God as the "lover of life" (Wisd. of Sol. 11:26) and in this way expresses an unending affirmation of reality. Jesus of Nazareth lived this unending affirmation. He drew to himself precisely those who lived on the fringes or were cast out, like women and children, prostitutes and collab-orators. He affirmed those who were everywhere rejected and compelled to reject themselves. It is from the background of this affirmation of life, even the life of those who were sick, disabled, or too weak to accomplish much, that one must see the understanding of the acceptance of suffering as it developed in Christianity. It is an attempt to see life as a whole as mean-ingful and to shape it as happiness. It is an eternal affirmation of temporal reality. The God who is the lover of life does not desire the suffering of people, not even as a pedagogical device, but instead their happiness.   — SU, 99–108

JESUS' DEATH

I want to begin this meditation on the day of Christ's death with my recollections of a religious service I took part in last year.

A small group of Christians, among them a few Catholic nuns and a large number of Spanish-speaking refugees, stood in front of the White House in Washington. The sun had come out; tourists were streaming by. Occasionally one would stop for a while or join us. We had chosen as our theme an old symbol of Christian piety, the contemplation of the Stations of the Cross. Jesus is taken captive, he is interrogated, he is crowned with thorns, he collapses for the first time under the weight of the cross, and so on, until his death by torture. A speaker reminded us that this was the day of Christ's death, that on this same day eleven years earlier Martin Luther King Jr. was shot, and that a few weeks ago Oscar Romero, the archbishop of San Salvador, was murdered as he was celebrating Mass.

As the different stations of Christ's suffering were named, large placards illustrating the life of the people in El Salvador today were held up. For the text "He is taken prisoner" a photograph showing the *Guardia Civil,* the police, shoving peasants into a jeep was shown. Passersby and those of us taking part in the service saw women searching in a village for their young sons who had been abducted and probably murdered. For the text "He collapses for the first time under the weight of the cross," we saw a body riddled with bullets lying by the roadside. Under the inscription "He is whipped," we saw modern instruments of torture, among them the *picana* — an electrical torture device — and the water bucket in which the victim's head is held until he almost drowns.

The commentary was brief and sober. We prayed together, mostly traditional prayers. A photograph of Oscar Romero lay on the grass. An allusion was made to Pontius Pilate, who sits in the White House and washes his hands because he allegedly has nothing to do with all this. There was reflection, shock, pain. There were the agitated faces of the young refugees from Uruguay, Chile, Argentina, who had had experiences like these or just barely escaped having them. We were a small group, forty at the most. Thousands of busy workers and tourists passed by.

Later, in keeping with my own German traditions, I went to one of those immense neo-Gothic cathedrals to hear a concert of religious music. I sat among people who were better dressed than the group in front of the White House. I listened to baroque music in an atmosphere that I felt to be unthinking and devoid of emotion.

These two experiences of Good Friday were worlds apart, but at the end of that day I knew quite clearly where I belonged: on the street, not in the solemn church with its thin music, not under the shadow of the organ's tones. I belonged with that unrespected group that was not enjoying Good Friday esthetically but making the connections between it and present-day suffering. This is what it must have been like for the first Christians, I thought: a fringe group of outsiders, looked down upon by others, out of place in the official cults that were all devoted to sanctioning the power of the state, to glorifying the marvelous lives of the high and mighty, to keeping quiet about the oppressed lives of the masses. Today, those masses make up two-thirds of the world's population, and they are condemned to the same poverty and hunger now as they were then. I use the biblical designation for them: "the poor."

I think we can understand Christ's death only if we see the torture and execution that he suffered (and that we euphemize by calling the "passion") in the light of what is happening today. We can understand it only if we share in the battle to the death and in the pain that people are forced to suffer today in the name of justice.

It is not a matter of indifference whether or not we make this connection between Christ and the present-day situation. If we fail to make it, we are simply denying Jesus. We have to "draw him into our flesh," as Luther put it, into our historical flesh, into what is significant to people today. When Luther used this expression, his meaning was a clearly polemical one. It is aimed at those who do not want to draw Christ into their concrete, everyday flesh but want to spiritualize him so that he has nothing to do with *campesinos* being tortured to death in El Salvador. To draw him into the flesh means to bring him out of abstraction, out of the distance, out of mere intellectual preoccupation into the reality we have to live with.

He concerned himself with political reality, even then. Jesus gave his own life because he loved the poor. Had he loved the rich above all and only them, as we like to assume for utterly transparent reasons, then he would not have had to die. The great confrontation at the end of his life, the one that took him to Jerusalem where the powers that be had their stronghold, makes sense only if we see it as a confrontation in the interest of the poor. Jesus' political base, his following, was stronger in Galilee. There he could heal the sick, feed the hungry, and spread his message. But the real illness afflicting the people was located elsewhere; if they were truly going to satisfy their hunger, they needed a far more radical redistribution of the goods of this earth. Words alone were apparently not enough to make his message comprehensible.

Jesus is a man who gave his life for love of the poor. He gave his life away instead of hoarding it and making it secure. He threw it away, or so his family thought, and they also thought he was more or less mad. What they were right about was that he did what he did of his own free will.

There was no compulsion, in the sense that God had created Jesus to suffer and now he was obliged to do what was pre-ordained for him. That is bad theology: it overlooks the element of freedom. We might say that God had created Jesus to love — that is, created him for the greatest freedom imaginable. And this love led, as every serious love does, to suffering. It led Jesus to the center of power, to Jerusalem. From the provinces to the capital, from the rural synagogue to the temple, from the poor to the rich. It led him from obscurity to visibility.

A political song from Chile says that to love means not to hide your face. Jesus hid his face less and less. In the end, what he was became completely visible. They tortured him so long that there was nothing opaque, nothing partial, nothing cautious, nothing reserved left in him. Then he could say: it is accomplished. Here I am, a human being for others.

A new quality of human existence had been achieved, something for which there were no words in the language of that time. Jesus' secret, his power, his refusal to hide his face, had to be given some kind of name. The expression that Jesus' first friends found and that, in their opinion, came closest to expressing what they meant was "Son of God," "Son of the Highest." How could anyone give that name to a political criminal who had just been tortured to death? A Roman centurion stood by the cross on Good Friday and "saw" who this Jesus was. "Truly this man was the son of God." What did he mean by that? What I think he meant was: this man did not hide his face. This man gave his life because he loved the poor. This man was as near to God as a son is to his father. He has made visible the truth we have done nothing but talk about. He was the truth: light, water, the bread of life. This, at any, rate, is what his followers meant when they called him God's son.

Jesus lived without protection. That is not a statement of faith but a simple statement of fact. He renounced the protection that a family can offer. He did not want the protection that property can give. He chose to keep silent rather than make use of the protection his eloquence could have given him. He explicitly rejected the protection that weapons and armies can provide. When Peter tried to defend him when he was taken captive, he said: "Put your sword, back, for all who draw the sword will die by the sword. Or do you think that I cannot appeal to my Father who would promptly send more than twelve legions of angels to my defense?" (Matt. 26:52–53). In the Roman army, a legion usually consisted of six thousand men. The term is used here to stand symbolically for an infinitely large number. If Jesus had wanted protection, he could have asked God for it and let God protect him. But he does not ask God for protection. He lives and acts without protection. The officials in power treat him like a dangerous criminal who is likely to resist with violence, but he could have been captured easily in broad daylight in the temple where he taught without protection and without giving a thought to fleeing. "It was at this time that Jesus said to the crowds, 'Am I a brigand, that you had to set out to capture me with swords and clubs? I sat teaching in the Temple day after day and you never laid hands on me'" (Matt. 26:55–56).

Jesus lived without protection. When his vulnerability became visible, when he rejected the natural response of striking back when attacked, when he refused to hope for the intervention of a higher power, at that point his disciples left him and fled. They apparently could not tolerate vulnerability; if that was the only alternative, they preferred violence; they preferred to be armed; at the very least they preferred to be able to make threats.

But Jesus lived without protection. He did not just put up with his vulnerability; he chose it voluntarily. He chose to live without weapons, without violence, and without the protection that force — even if only in the form of threats — can offer. Jesus was not armed, and he did not seek out the arms of others to hide behind. This kind of vulnerability has a provocative effect.

This is the very effect that Jesus' disciples came to feel. And this is why they began one day to call this man who had lived nonviolently among them, without protection and without weapons, the "Son of God." This was an affirmation of Jesus' way of living without weapons. "He is the Son of God" did not mean: he has at his disposal all the weapons, all the legions, all the threats, all that he needs to destroy an enemy. It means just the opposite of "God with us" on the field-pack buckles of any army.

Jesus' vulnerability, his renunciation of violence as the core of our perception of him as the son, friend, heir, manifestor, realizer of God implies an understanding of God different from the one generally accepted today. If the disciples were right when they called him the "Son of God" and if this expression reveals an essential truth, then the word "God" must have a meaning totally different from the one we usually give it.

If Jesus is the one who does not hide his face, then God cannot very well continue to hide his either. If Jesus lives and acts nonviolently, then God too will have to manage without violence. If Jesus became free of fear, then God too has to become free of fear — which is to say, he will have to renounce force of arms. It is customary in our society — whether we believe in God or not — to worship power, to honor strength, to favor the use of force, especially when force takes the form of violence perpetrated by the state and the police. We are much more subject to the spell of violence than we suspect. To live means to live without protection, not to hide. But we hide our faces from those who are starving; and we show them instead the legions of destruction we hold at the ready.

As more and more people came to see the nonviolent and unprotected man from Nazareth as the Son of God and began to call him the Son of God, the understanding of God changed. John expressed this by saying that Jesus makes the invisible God known or interprets him. The operative word here is "exegesis"; Jesus is the exegesis of God. "No one has ever seen God; it is the only Son, who is nearest to the Father's heart, who has made him known" (John 1:18). Christ makes visible the God that we want to see but cannot see, makes him visible so that we can know anew who God is and where we can search for him. Christ interprets God to be love that gives itself freely.

God does not want to protect himself or keep himself remote. God renounced violence and the kind of intervention that those in power practice. God does not make use of violence. In Jesus Christ, God disarmed himself. God surrendered himself without protection and without arms to those who keep crying for more and more protection and arms. In Jesus Christ, God renounced violence. And of course he did this unilaterally, without waiting for us to lay down our weapons first. In Christ, God disarmed unilaterally. He took the first step. He did not wait for others, insisting that they be the first to lay down their weapons. In Christ, he began unilaterally, on his own side, to renounce the threat of violence.

Not long ago on television I saw a leader of the Protestant church speak on the question: "Arms Buildup or Disarmament: Where Does the Church Stand?" He spoke primarily about military requirements, and when the reporter interviewing him pressed him for a theological perspective, he responded that from a theological point of view we are all guilty before God. He said, as I recall, that we are all guilty whether we possess weapons or not. The first thing that came to his mind theologically was guilt. When Protestant church leaders stress above all else in disarmament debates that we are all sinners, what they are doing is denying the existence of a God who refuses to make threats and rejects the use of violence.

If the most essential element of Christian faith is sin and not our capacity for love, if the first thing that should come to our minds in church and in our religious life is our impotence, our weakness, our guilt, our repeated failures, then the die is already cast. Then we cultivate our own fears and coddle our own need for security. We deny that human beings are capable of making peace; we abandon the unarmed Christ and run away just as the disciples did when Jesus was taken captive and when it became clear that protection and weapons were useless now. We are tempted to look for other masters who offer more protection and security.

The old vicious circle takes this form: we are weak and we feel weak. We are afraid and we teach others to be afraid. We seek safety — that is, we wall ourselves in and hide behind the armor plate of power, hide in the control towers of devastation, feel weak again, and therefore feel compelled to press the button.

Christ broke out of this vicious circle in which we still live, this vicious circle of weakness, fear, need for protection, need for security, need for violence. It is not true, he told us, that you are weak. You can do whatever you want if you have faith. You are strong; you are beautiful. You do not need to build any walls to hide behind. You can live without armaments. Because you are strong, you can put the neurotic need for security behind you. You do not need to defend your life like a lunatic. For love of the poor, Jesus says, you can give your life away and spread it around. The mechanism that runs its course from weakness to a need for security to violence is unsound. God is in you. You do not need to protect yourself. It is possible to live without violence and without weapons.

—WL, 91–92, 94–98

ON LIVING RESURRECTION, PART 1

There is hardly any other article of belief with which people today have greater problems than with the resurrection. When a young journalist once called me up and wanted to know whether Jesus really had risen from the dead, I was puzzled by this very old question. He explained it to me: theologians mostly talk around it, but he couldn't go to his editor with that! Now did Jesus really rise on Easter, or is the whole thing just a fairy tale? What would change for you, I asked in return, if the answer were yes or no? Great astonishment on his part: That would certainly put the foundation of belief into question. I stuck with my question: Assume Jesus did not come forth from the grave — after all, there are no valid proofs for it. Witnesses who saw him, male and female, were all, as we know, believers, partisans, sympathizers, thus by no means objective observers. What does that change for those who believe in him? Or for those who go with him, who feel themselves supported by his truth? I think nothing at all changes, came the answer.

Assuming Jesus was only apparently dead and was revived, would that change my relation to this Jesus? Assuming further that everything in the Bible is literally true, would there then be more Christians? Would Christians be more credible then, and would they look a little more redeemed? I think not. I found the question, which was posed after a scholarly discussion that has lasted for over two hundred years, to be somewhat off the mark. One result of this discussion is the unprovable character of the resurrection. Supposing photography had existed then, the film would have been blank. I gave the journalist two reasons why I had no desire to discuss the resurrection on this level.

The first reason is the cross, which may not be separated from the resurrection if one wants to keep to the meaning of the matter. Belief in the resurrection roots us in ancient history and in our own history. Easter does not celebrate a departure into a posthistory which has finally been attained, something following historical suffering. It celebrates history itself, this emergence from not being free. Without the early history recounted in the Hebrew Bible, the departure of the children of Israel from the house of slavery in Egypt, one cannot understand the departure of Jesus from the house of the dead.

The other reason is my own life, which I do not want to separate from the death and life of Jesus, nor from the defeat and victory of the life of God. Easter is either existential, or else it says nothing at all — and is rightfully commercialized.

Whether apparent death, resuscitation, and breaking through the laws of nature are a secure foundation for that which occurred two thousand years ago in Palestine, I do not know. But I am completely certain that this kind of discussion is a clever diversion from something else, namely, from the judicial murder of the poor wretch from Nazareth. What we know objectively is that he — like many before and after him — was tortured to death slowly and extremely cruelly. He could, as I said, have avoided this through flight, withdrawal into privacy, transcendental meditation, or other modes of escaping reality. Instead he stuck with the cause, faithful to the love of those whose rights and possessions had been taken, the "last," as he liked to call them. For these last, for those who were regarded as the dregs, he, with female and male friends, developed a new manner of living. He did not want to have it better than the poorest. Therefore he lived without violence and without protection from violence.

Then as today that was not allowed. The consequences from the Imperium toward this attempt at another life were brutal, just like today. Archbishop Oscar Romero, a friend of Jesus, was also "crucified," murdered by the helpers of the state power as he celebrated Mass. The approximately thirty thousand people who annually celebrate the day of his death call again and again: "Oscar Romero lives! He is with us. He is resurrected in his people. He stands by us." Is that a fairy tale which the people cling to only because they are poor and ignorant? Or is that the truth of their lives, for which they are prepared to live, fight, and even die? In the prayers and songs, in the marches and protests from the distant land whose coffee we drink, the resurrection becomes visible.

The resurrection cannot be discussed in isolation, as if it had nothing to do with the cross. As if Jesus would in any case, even if he had died of old age, have gotten the benefit of this wonder drug. If we keep before our eyes what this puzzling phrase "resurrected from the dead" says, then the reality "cross" belongs to it: whoever lives in love has to reckon with contempt, abuse, discrimination, even with death. In this other way of living, the resurrection is already visible long before death. Jesus believed above all — and for all — in a life before death. The resurrection, this spark of life, was already in him. And only because of this God-in-him were they unable to kill him. It simply did not function. Even today the powerful do not succeed in extinguishing this love of justice, this sustained interest in the "last."

If we ask ourselves whether Jesus as a clinically dead person was resuscitated, that is a speculation for our scientific curiosity. It does not affect us at all. False thinking — whether fairy tales or facts — occupy us completely from outside and keep us from ourselves. More correctly stated, the question reads: "Is Jesus dead or is he still alive? Does he still bring something about? Does he change people's lives? Can one still say, 'Jesus lives, and in him I live also'?"

Only those who themselves have been resurrected can actually celebrate Easter. Goethe said this in Faust's Easter walk:

"They celebrate the Resurrection /For they themselves today are risen." And then Faust details where and from what oppression and truncation of life the people come:

> From airless rooms in huddled houses
> From drudgery at counters and benches
> From under cumbrous roofs and gables
> From crowded, suffocating alleys
> From the mouldering dimness of the churches
> All are brought forth into brightness.

Are there still today experiences of liberation that are more than individual? That would be a serious question after the festival of the resurrection. Experiences like those from El Salvador and other countries of the oppressed world occur to me. What about in my own country, Germany? I shall again go to the Easter march which still at least identifies the cross, from the terrorism of low-level flights to grandiose transactions with exported weapons. The number of those who in this way experience a piece of resurrection from present-day death is becoming negligible. But on that first Easter morning, too, not many were present.   — TS, 104–8

ON LIVING RESURRECTION, PART 2

Let me try to present my theological interpretation of resurrection; it takes its origin from the biblical texts, but it is nourished and strengthened by other sources too. So I try to read the Bible in the light of Joe Hill,* who never died, and in the light of his brothers and sisters.

---

*Note: Joe Hill (d. 1915), a martyr of the American labor movement, was memorialized in a famous ballad: "I dreamed I saw Joe Hill last night. . . . " — Ed.

Nothing is so primal an expression of the Christian faith as the story of the resurrection. Christ has risen from the dead: that was and is a message of life-transforming power. It is the center of the faith to which people have clung even under shattering conditions. There is such a thing as the reconciliation of estranged life; there is a victory over death and injustice. When in the Easter Eve liturgy we cry to each other "Christ is risen! He is risen indeed!" then we are crying "Liberation!" and we are one with tormented and shattered people, and one with the poor. "He is risen," we say, and mean: we shall be filled, we love our mother the earth, we are building peace with the whole of our lives. We are beating swords into ploughshares. The power of what resurrection means must be felt in our own lives. We must again take possession of these words — resurrection, life from the dead, righteousness, and justice — recognizing them as true on the basis of our own experience. Once we have given a name to our experience, we can describe our lives in the framework of the great symbols of our tradition: we too were in Egypt; we too know what Exodus means; we too know the jubilation of becoming free — of resurrection from the dead. Only the Christian experience we have made a part of our lives can be passed on, can be communicated to other people. But this power of the resurrection is veiled and remains unreal if we view Christ's resurrection in exclusive terms. If we make it an exclusive privilege of Christ's, then we miss its meaning, which is inclusive and means us all. To say that he is risen only has a point if we know that we too shall rise from the death in which we are now existing. He has left death behind him. But the decisive thing about this message is not an end in itself, not a complete, self-contained item of information.

There is a danger of falling victim to a theological heresy which the feminist theologian Mary Daly has aptly called "Christolatry." If we venerate Christ's resurrection without sharing in it, we are making an idol out of Christ, a fetish, which does not touch our own desolation. Sometimes I think that Christ is so homeless in the churches today because he finds worshipers there, but no friends. Too much adoration, too little fellowship. Because, admiring Christ doesn't mean following him. Kierkegaard made that very clear to us. The worship of Christ without participation in his life, his sufferings, and his death is the prevailing form of religion, at least in the first world. There are slogans — "One way!" "Jesus loves you!" "Take Jesus!" — none of which offer anything with which to counter the prevailing individualism. These have a mass effect, but they are really harmless, a pattered formula, "Lord, Lord," which does not express what that lordship means. Words like Jesus, obedience, love, faith, resurrection, remain completely untranslated in this religiosity, as if their meaning was above and apart from time, something once and for all; indeed it is not even felt necessary to say more precisely who Jesus is and why he is so important. Instead of being connected with experiences of liberation, steps toward righteousness and peace, he is set above reality as an authority. The authoritarian character of this piety justifies us in talking here about a kind of Christo-fascism.

It is the religion with which the usual kind of fascism can run its course, which unconsciously and helplessly works for fascism, by glorifying dependency; which believes itself to be nonpolitical, but which really confirms forms of political power. The mania for adoring or worshipping power is not cured by writing "Jesus" on one's banners instead of Hitler or Mussolini. The Christ of Christo-fascism doesn't suffer; he was never poor; or, if he was, that was unimportant — something purely external. He didn't perform his miracles in expectation of the kingdom of God and organize people toward that goal; his actions were purely individual acts of help. This Jesus, in fact,

loves you and you and you, but not us all. The Christ of the
Christo-facists ended up on the cross, not for political reasons but for internal religious ones, because that was what his
Father wanted. In this context the Bible isn't read as a ma-
terialistic book, which takes the human body seriously — its
hunger, for example, and its society; instead it is idealistically
spiritualized. The human-being-who-was-God acts in our stead.
Worship, adoration, idolatry is the relationship to him which
we can develop, not discipleship and participation.

But believing in Christ's resurrection doesn't mean heroic
idolatry. It is precisely this which we can learn from the song
about Joe Hill. I never died, said he. I am not dead. But these
statements depend on his friends, on the people who carry on
his cause. Resurrection as something purely objective, as a mere
fact which would be true even without us, has no meaning.
It would then only be a theological materialization under a
positivist perspective of the world. The biblical witnesses are
as far from this Christolatry and materialization as the people
who sang about Joe Hill. Joe Hill, he in himself, he *a se,* to
use a scholastic term, is dead. If individualism is our ultimate
and most profound category for human beings, then we cannot
understand what the resurrection is really about.

But anthropologically there is nothing which could be called
Christ alone, he in himself. We are a part of Jesus Christ,
and he belongs to our human existence, which cannot be defined by the limits of our body or in line with the uniqueness
of our personalities, but through our social relationships. As
people, we can be defined better through our relationships than
through our substance. Our nature is a living relationship to
others, a relationship resting on mutual help and sustained by
an elemental need for communication. It is only in the capitalist
concept of the person that we are reduced to monads whose

relationship to the world is expressed in having, consuming, and dominating.

We must free the idea of resurrection from the stranglehold of individualism. This also means that resurrection was not an event, an individual, isolated event which took place once, two thousand years ago. It must rather be understood as a process and it happens afresh, again and again, that people who were dead before rise again from the dead. Some people have already risen from the dead; if we remember them, we nourish our own hope of resurrection. This hope itself is unproven and unprovable. It is a genuine act of faith. The only possible proof of Christ's resurrection and our own would be a changed world, a world a little closer to the kingdom of God.

Resurrection gives us the beginning of the kingdom, not its completion. The pain of the unfulfilled promise is still with us. Christ bears the stigmata of his crucifixion on his body; in this sense the tradition itself witnesses to the difference between the resurrection and the kingdom of God, when the wounds are healed. So when we talk about liberation, we too mean an uncompleted process. By using this expression we are talking about the struggle for liberation which is itself liberating. We are not talking about freedom as a gift which we have received once and for all. In the concept of a permanent liberation, the cross and the resurrection are both present.

The resurrection is the symbol of faith. It is most profoundly encoded and it resists decipherment. Different periods have attempted different translations of this symbol. Whereas bourgeois theology stressed the individual dimension, the new theology which we are working on will stress the social dimension of the mystery. We link resurrection with liberation because our deepest need is not personal immortality but a life before death for everyone.

But is there a life before death of this kind? How could we describe it? Where does resurrection and liberation then take place? I believe that the strongest sign of the new life is solidarity. Where there is solidarity there is resurrection. When we break the neutrality of silence and abandon our complicity with injustice, the new life begins. People who earlier were invisible and forgotten become self-assured and find their own language. They stand up for their rights, and this revolt, this rebellion, is a sign of resurrection. I should like here to describe three elements of the new life: the new language, new forms of lifestyle, and new communities.

When zones of liberation emerge, people begin to talk a new language, in which the words "mine" and "yours" lose their meaning. One can make a whole list of words which belong to the language of the oppressor and are then replaced. In June 1976, schoolchildren in Soweto, South Africa, protested against the conditions in which they were living. The government had ordered that teaching in black schools should be given in Afrikaans. Mathematics, history, and geography were to be taught in Afrikaans, a language which black teachers are as little proficient in as the black ghetto children. In those days, fifteen thousand schoolchildren marched through Soweto in protest. On their banners and placards was written: "Do not force Afrikaans down our throats!" "Our teachers can't teach in Afrikaans!" "Afrikaans — the language of the oppressor!"

I believe we have all learned the language of the oppressor. As a child I learned Nazi German. Many of my North American friends were brought up with the cultural imperialism of Donald Duck. Our mass education takes place in the medium of advertising, which sullies every human emotion, because it presupposes that everything is for sale. Tenderness is something which the mild soap of a particular firm gives the skin. If anyone talks about the healthy, robust person, what he means is the person who is completely at the mercy of this power, who has surrendered his thinking and his feelings. We all grew up with the Afrikaans of the oppressor. We all have first to learn the language of liberation and, like every learning process, this one begins with a forgetting, a freeing from the mendacious language of children's television, the schools, and the churches.

God is defined in the Christian tradition as love, as "that very love with which we love one another," as St. Augustine says. But in the language of the oppressor, in the Afrikaans of advertising which beats in on us, the word "love" is the definition of the relationship between a person and his car. And even if we use this word more seriously, it is reduced to the relationship between two people, cut off from the world and time. In our corrupted language, it often means no more than "I'm OK, you're OK"; and this trivial middle-class game is increasingly passed off on us as "God," even theologically. We are only capable of a disturbed, privatistic interpretation of love, and forget that God is the love which, as Juan Segundo says, forms "human society in history." The new language, which is a sign of resurrection, will teach us that God "despite all our twisted and distorted images . . . is a God who is a society."

In this new language the existence of the individual will not have significance *in spite of* the senselessness of history and society, but *in accord with* history's meaning. The great educationalist Pestalozzi said at the beginning of the nineteenth century: "There is no God and there is no belief in God as long as the suffering caused by injustice does not stop." We cannot talk about God until we have become a part of the historical movement which ends suffering from injustice. We cannot talk about God until we have begun to be the agents, the subjects of this process of change called God.

The second thing I should like to mention is the new lifestyle which is lived in the islands of resurrection. A growing number of people are forming groups which are breaking with the old culture and rejecting its standards of education, career, income, and way of living. The simplest form of solidarity with the poor is what the French worker priests in the 1950s called "presence": to be present, to share the life of the underprivileged, to be beside them in the struggle, to fight with them, not for them. The radical character of Jesus is a model for different lifestyles like this. He ate and drank with whores; he gave up home and work; he developed a new language, which he and the poor found together and which was real for them, a very simple language of prayer and parable, which emerged from the context of their lives — the lives of the poor, the unemployed day-laborers, fishermen, and housewives. The grassroots congregations, which are growing up in Latin America and in some European countries too, are examples of the new lifestyle of the resurrection. The renunciation of middle-class privileges is part of this way of living. People work in cooperatives, that is to say, without the specific forms of estranged labor. The groups read the Gospels together and develop new forms of the spirituality of liberation, which rests on radical identification with the poor.

The new style of living, which we have first to search for, is connected with the new understanding of the surrender of our own lives. Surrender is both a spiritual and a political concept; the two experiences can no longer be separated from one another. To participate in the resurrection means that our lives don't lead toward what is dead, are not exposed to death's magnetic attraction. To be a Christian means that death is behind us. It no longer lies in wait for us. What awaits us is the love of which we are a part. As John says: "We know that we have passed out of death into life, because we love the brethren" (1 John 3:14). "Out of death" is a description of normal, natural life. We must imagine the normal life of ordinary, middle-class people as being shot through with death.

Its security is founded on dead capital; it acquires its mindless and inane joys from what is dead, from the possession and consumption of what is dead; its deepest anxieties are directed toward life's physical end. Possession, income, the kind of education that can be "exploited," career, and security are all supposed to cover up death; yet these things really only guarantee death's reality. By nature we live in death. It is only when we become capable of loving that we have "passed out of death into life" and no longer need to fear, and no longer need to love death's symbols — money, career, power. When death is behind us — which means the fear of death and the greed for what is dead — then the love into which we grow is ahead of us.

This brings me to the third sign of resurrection — the new forms of community. To build up community, to gain friends for the common cause, is not something which can be regulated by a division of labor, so that some Christians work as missionaries and others don't. The new life is lived only as a shared and extended life. The resurrection of Joe Hill is described in the simple words:

> What they forgot to kill
> Went on to organize.

Jesus sent out his friends to build the kingdom of God. He gave them exact information about the way they were to behave, such as having no shoes, having no second garment to change into, always going in twos. Where their organization was concerned, the most important instruction he gave them was the anti-hierarchical one:

> You know that the rulers of the Gentiles lord it over them,
> and their great men exercise authority over them. It shall
> not be so among you; but whoever would be great among
> you must be your servant, and whoever would be first

among you must be our slave; even as the Son of man
came not to be served but to serve, and to give his life
as a ransom for many. (Matt. 20:25–28)

The reduction of privileges and domination is one criterion
for a liberated life. Jesus washed his disciples' feet — another
sign of solidarity. The value of a member of the group is as-
sessed, not according to his natural gifts or his social position
in the group, but according to the question of how this member
meets people's needs.

What does resurrection mean for us? It means forgetting the
language of the oppressor; it means a change in lifestyle; and it
means new community. All these experiences which people have
when they get involved with the cross are simultaneously political and theological changes. The radicalization is not divisible.
To become more devout works out in practice in society as becoming more radical. Political radicalization also means new
spirituality. I think it is a catastrophic mistake if in the Christian tradition we bring about a division of labor between those
who fight and those who pray, those who risk action designed
to change the world and those who seek strength and renewal
in prayer and reading the Bible. Struggle and contemplation belong together. A division of labor in this central self-expression
of faith is deadly; it makes the people who fight blind and brutal, and the people who pray sentimental and deaf to the cries
without.   — CL, 84–93

RESISTANCE

Resistance is how human beings who are members of the white
bourgeoisie — those who normally participate in oppression

and profit from exploitation — participate in liberation struggles. Doing theology in the first world has more often the meaning of resistance than of liberation struggle; to resist is probably the adequate form of struggle for those who are Christians in Egypt.

Theology of liberation starts with a new translation of the old word *soteria,* which originally meant rescue, deliverance from danger of dying or from prison. The tradition usually translated it as salvation. Now we change the translation (which is what theologians ought to do) and say: *Soteria* is liberation. Christ is the liberator. Jesus' message of the Kingdom of God is to be taken as a message about the construction of a world in which justice and henceforth peace will be possible. The liberator is not seen, as the Savior often is, descending from above to take us from a bad to a good position. The liberator is expression and part of the movement for liberation. We get into the process of liberation in his spirit and with his strengthening.

Whereas salvation is the deed of a totally other, who deals with unsaved people to save them, liberation is cooperation between Christ and the people. At this point process theology is very helpful in understanding the concept of liberation. It would be a betrayal of our deepest expectations even to wait for a mere gift or to dream of a sudden wonder. Nobody can give liberation to someone else; liberation cannot be bestowed on someone, neither on a class nor on a people nor on the oppressed half of humanity. To participate in the struggle is a necessary presupposition of the concept of liberation....

I don't want to polarize resistance over against liberation. Theology of liberation does not exclude theology of resistance. Maybe the emphasis on resistance is only a special case of liberation theology in a frozen situation. Resistance and liberation then would be related as in the French experiences of resistance against the Germans: *La Resistance* beginning in 1940 led to *La Liberation* of 1945.

What we could learn from historical resistance movements has to do with the personal experience of people who try to live in "hope against hope." That is to say, they do not ground their hope only in the objective maturity of a given situation. Whereas Marxists sometimes seem to make a fetish out of the objective maturity of a historical situation, Christians could in faithfulness to their tradition overcome the spell of the expectation of the perfect revolutionary situation and work right now without postponing the Messiah. They should know a little about the tensions in the New Testament between the "already there" and the "not yet"; they are in danger of losing their hope and exchanging the not yet into a never. Others of us enjoy too much the "already there" of the small group where peace and strength are to be found. They are in danger of forgetting about the not yet.

There is no liberation without the subjective experience of resistance: Of doing what you have to do without asking about success. I remember some demonstrations in the early fifties against the German rearmament and integration into the Western Alliance. We were few; we had with us a lot of elderly women in shabby coats — who were nicknamed *Friedenstanten* (peace aunts). What I learned in those years was that sometimes one has to do things simply to maintain one's integrity. You cannot get hold of liberation like a gift. In that case it would lose its freeing character. But isn't it also true that there is no resistance that is not ultimately grounded in the hope for liberation? Are there not many paths between resistance and liberation?

There is a certain anti-Protestant point in the thesis that salvation is liberation. Theologians of liberation are critical of the prevailing anthropological pessimism inside of Protestantism. "Mit unserer Macht ist nichts getan," as Luther sang — With our might nothing can be done. Take for example the concept of original sin. In liberation theology one finds an emphasis on the contingency of original sin; it once came into this world and therefore can disappear also from a more human society than the one we have now. Sin originated under certain circumstances. If greed and lust for power are no longer structurally rewarded in a given society, then change is possible. This is a good example of the differing uses of certain theological concepts. They can be used in a repressive, but also possibly in a liberating way.

We all know how a secularized faith in original sin blends easily with one of the most important cultural beliefs of late capitalism, namely, the ideology of powerlessness. "What can you do? You can't beat City Hall." Again, it is anthropological pessimism to assume that it is natural to human beings to compete, to offend and to oppress, and that we'll never be free from these inbuilt characteristics of the human race. When we buy into this myth, we agree with a prevailing understanding of history that is totally anti-Christian. This dominant reading of history tells us there is nothing you can even hope for; sometimes this group is on top, sometimes another one. There is an eternal repetition of the sameness, namely, the meanness in all of us. We know all too well that we are not in heaven and that not all is possible; but by remembering it so well we forget the message of the New Testament, the center of which is the radical phrase, "All is possible to one who has faith" (Mark 9:23).

According to this basically pessimistic understanding of our nature, history, and humanity's role in it, we limit the meaning of Christ's resurrection, too. We take it as an individual event that only concerns Jesus. We separate Jesus from us. We buy into the dominating concept of history. We also tear apart

salvation and liberation, for we make out of salvation something above time, above this world, existing only within us. We
permanently postpone life. José Miranda talks about this postponing of life. "God is revealed only in the implacable 'now' of
the moral imperative of justice and love for all. To postpone the
kingdom, to postpone the Messiah is to prevent them from ever
being real." The Protestant separation of justification and sanc-
tification has theologically ensured this antimessianic program.
Our normal concept of history is anti-Christian. We are caught
by the basic capitalistic experiences of powerlessness, determination from the outside, uncontrollability of life. We do need
resistance over against the prevailing experience and ideology,
mutually enforced.   — "Resistance," 178–79, 180–81

BETWEEN CREATION AND RESISTANCE

With a view to resistance, I would like to reflect once more on
the concept of creation. Is there an interrelation between faith
in creation and our becoming resisters? How might we finally
bring together the biblical traditions of creation and liberation?
The connectedness of the two concepts becomes visible when
we rid ourselves of an exclusively past-oriented understanding
of creation and fully accept that creation is unfinished, that it
continues.

We may distinguish three biblically based forms of creation.
The first creation that brought us into being is visualized in
Genesis 1. In contemplating this text, I have always found a certain consolation in the knowledge that the winds, the waters,
the earth, the air, the fish, and the birds were there before we
humans were called into being. Being, as it is depicted in Genesis, means being-in-relation, living in togetherness. When I think
about death, and that means contemplating my own death, I

feel part of this planet called earth. When I pass away, the winds and the waters, the earth and the air, the fish and the birds, and all the other animals will continue to exist. Why then should I fear death? It is because of the interrelatedness of the created universe that Francis of Assisi was able to speak about death as "our sister." To talk this way is the greatest affirmation of creation we can make, for it means that we have integrated death into life. Then we are able to see our little beings as part of the great Being to which we will return, sister to Sister Death, child to Mother Earth, brother to Brother Sun, drop to the great Waters, flame to the Light.

I am afraid, however, that human beings today are a part of nonbeing, that our unrelatedness is catapulting us into undoing creation and all that lives on the small planet earth. I fear that nothingness will supersede being, that the bomb is in our hearts as well as in our hands, and that we hate creation because we have chosen to live under the bomb. No generation in history was ever able to say no to creation as we can. No generation has heretofore been able to kill not just Jesus Christ again and again but God the creator, the Being-in-relation. We may fool ourselves with superficial Christian slogans about the "Eternal God," but there will not be any heavenly father or mother or creator after the nuclear holocaust, after the final solution.

Traditional Christians sometimes misconstrue the concept of creation in a fatalistic way. And those on the far right are prone to manipulate this sensibility, claiming that God is in charge of everything and that should he decide to undo his creation no love of mothers for their children, no rational behavior on the part of reasonable beings, no resistance against the strategies of death will stop him. Political leaders who appropriate this theology and talk seriously about Armageddon disclose their secret lust for power over life and death and pave the way for military planners who account for megadeaths in their war scenarios.

This pseudo-religious ideology is heresy, disguised as pious surrender to the will of God. It mixes up God and Satan until they are indistinguishable. Is it Satan who wants to terminate creation, or is it God? To the purveyors of military fascism, it hardly matters; for them, the unifying concept that counts is power. Power is worthy of adoration, nothing else. And it is power that triumphs when right-wing Christians subordinate themselves to the "princes of this world" in a seemingly devout surrender to the will of an ill-defined God. The power of those who command the military-industrial complex, who steer us toward death, is kept intact by Christians who cry out "His will, not ours" as they embrace the nuclear option. Theirs is a religious ideology in which an authoritarian God enters into a nightmarish alliance with the unconscious wish to eradicate the cities of the enemy or, in the Pentagon's own language, to decapitate their leaders as one decapitates a chicken. In this ideology God does not live where justice and love bloom; God reigns as the supreme superpower. In this ideology the concept of creation is severed from notions of love and justice and is thus transformed into an expression of the absolute right of the superpower to do what it wants with its subjects.

If we want to respond to creation differently, with loving care for all that lives on earth, and if we aspire to become what we were meant to be, that is, co-creators, created in God's image, then we must realize that creation refers not only to our origin but to our future as well. The creation that began with the first creation is unfinished.

The second creation that brought us into being is revealed in the Exodus story as the time when the people of God passed through the Red Sea out of slavery and into the land of freedom. The second creation happens in history. There is a great exodus in progress today out of the Egypt of militarism and dependency into a land where peace and justice may embrace each other. To remember our second creation in history, our flight from Egypt and the slave house, is to think about all the peoples, such as the Salvadorans, who are currently struggling to make their long and painful way out of the Egypt of their oppressors. The second creation is also not yet finished. Each generation must define its understanding of freedom in a new way. Today the people of Europe offer a new definition of freedom: Freedom means freedom from nuclear weapons; life means living without bombs, and we will not be free as long as we live with them.

There is a third creation that the Bible talks about symbolically as our baptism into death and rebirth in Jesus Christ. The "new woman" and the "new man" come into being in a process of death and resurrection:

> Do you not know that all of us who have been baptized into Christ Jesus were baptized into his death? We were buried therefore with him by baptism into death, so that as Christ was raised from the dead by the glory of the Father, we too might walk in the newness of life. For if we have been united with him in a death like his, we shall certainly be united with him in a resurrection like his. We know that our old self was crucified with him so that...we might no longer be enslaved to sin. (Rom. 6:3–6)

To be reborn we have to die with Christ, which means that the old self is crucified with Christ. Who is the "old man" or the "old woman" who has to die? It is the old being: the egotistic, the self-concerned, the apolitical human being. It is often the pious self caught up in a form of spirituality that glorifies individualism. But the sinful self referred to by the apostle Paul may just as easily be the secular individualist who affirms the decency and goodness of his own life while blinding himself to the scope of concrete suffering in our world.

The "old being" who must die is not only the egocentric; she is also the powerless human being who feels incapable of changing anything in her world. She is, as Paul puts it, "enslaved to sin." She is a slave to the powers who prepare the nuclear holocaust, a slave to injustice and the destruction of the earth. Egotism and powerlessness are the main characteristics of the old being.

The new human being is born in the resurrection of Christ. He and she are empowered to fight death and those who hold us under the sway of death. The new human being in Christ is a resister, a revolutionary. She knows that for which she lives and gives her life. He is a fighter for the city of God. The new human being is a loving being who participates in the three forms of creation as a co-creator. He and she are committed to the renewal of the earth, to our liberation from bondage, and to resistance against death and all the powers of death. The third creation is as unfinished as the other two. All three creations continue still.

We cannot afford to have a naive trust in the first creation. The "fate of the earth" in a nuclear age, which Jonathan Schell has illuminated so well for us in a book by that name, is not something about which we may rest assured because it lies in God's hands. The fate of the earth is equally in our hands, and only a community of resisters may prevent the extermination of humankind and the rest of creation. The God who created the universe, including our planet, and who delivered us from slavery is the same God who raises the dead to new life, so that we who were dead and without hope might become resisters and lovers of life. "Lover of the living" is an old name for God (Wisd. of Sol. 11:26). So shall it be our name for evermore.

—TWTL, 162–65

WE GO WITH HIM

But within the critique of the man who comes into the world and regards himself as God there lies still another question which can be called that regarding Christolatry, or idolizing of Christ. Why do we need heroes, gurus, wise men, or leaders anyhow? How is someone who lived two thousand years ago supposed to be the decisive occurrence for everyone, those who live later and, in many speculations about Christ, also those who lived earlier? Do we really need a savior, a king, a conqueror, a redeemer? Someone who does everything that we cannot, who loves when we can no longer love, hopes when we give up, lives when we die? This question is difficult to answer, and I believe in fact that we need more for living than just ourselves. The individualism which lies behind the question must be criticized. But again the tradition of a christology from above is more of an impediment. We do not need another conqueror, judge, or hero. Nor is a redeemer needed if the word means that some overpowering person transplants me out of the miserable position in which I find myself into a good, unscathed other world without my cooperation. These caricatures of being saved through Christ surely cannot be what is intended!

"To redeem" in the Bible amounts to the same as to liberate or save or heal. Christ is not the superhero who suddenly and magically makes cancer or nuclear weapons go away. But he does free us from the fear of being possessed by evil, and he heals by taking away our anxiety which blocks our healing power. To redeem means to set free the power of God, "that of God" in us; therefore the redeemed are those who insist on their human dignity. "When I get to heaven," sang the black slaves in the South, "then I'm going to run around freely everywhere; no one will throw me out." The liberating Christ of these people kept their human dignity, their hunger and thirst for righteousness alive.

The goal of the Christian religion is not the idolizing of Christ, not Christolatry, but that we all "are in Christ," as the mystical expression goes, that we have a part in the life of Christ. This savior is a wounded healer, and he heals so that we may become as he is. Be as he is, laugh as he laughs, weep as he weeps. Heal the sick, even those who without knowing it have contracted the great neuroses of our society, who know no mercy with themselves and their children when they consent to the nuclear state and technologies inimical to life. To feed the hungry means to do away with militarism. To bless the children means to leave the trees standing for them.

Christolatry is the opposite of what it means to be "in Christ." Søren Kierkegaard practiced this distinction between those who esteem Christ and those who follow him. If I esteem him then I lift him ever higher and have nothing to do with him, I use my admiration to keep myself free of Christ. He is big, I am dependent on him, yet I do not want to go his way. But if I try to follow him, then he never calls to me saying, "Leave well enough alone; you can't do anything anyway. I have already settled everything once for all time." His language is completely different from that of the dogmaticians: "Come along," he says, and that above all. "Come along into God's kingdom — to our home country, where no one is beaten, no one is thrown out and shoved away. Look and see," he says to me and shows how the lame begin to walk. He does not say, "Close your eyes; I'll do everything."

My relationship to Christ is thus not that of a personality cult *à la* Joseph Stalin or Adolf Hitler. I am with him on the way, but here I must more correctly say "we," because that corresponds to my experience of resistance and working for God's kingdom. We who get involved in him and regard his as the right way are with him on the way. We do not marvel; we go with him. He is our "firstborn brother," as Paul says. Latin American devotion expresses this nicely: less is being said today about Christ the King (*Cristo rey*), and more about *compañero cristo*.

In a certain sense the word "Christ" thus expresses a collective meaning. If Jesus of Nazareth was the poor man from Galilee who was tortured to death, then Christ is that which cannot be destroyed, which came into the world with him and lives through us in him. When I say Christ, I always think also of Francis of Assisi and Hildegard of Bingen and Martin Luther King Jr., and of Ita Ford, the American nun who was murdered in El Salvador — as well as of all resistance fighters who are sitting in prison today. Christ is a name which for me expresses solidarity, hence suffering with, struggling with. Christ is the mysterious power which was in and which continues on and sometimes makes us into "fools in Christ," who, without hope of success and without an objective, share life with others. Share bread, shelter, anxiety, and joy. Jesus' attitude toward life was that it cannot be possessed, hoarded, safeguarded. What we can do with life is to share it, pass it along, get it as a gift, and give it on.   — TS, 91–93

HE NEEDS YOU

He needs you
that's all there is to it
without you he's left hanging
goes up in dachau's smoke
is sugar and spice in the baker's hands
gets revalued in the next stock market crash
he's consumed and blown away

used up
without you

Help him
that's what faith is
he can't bring it about
his kingdom
couldn't then couldn't later can't now
not at any rate without you
and that is his irresistible appeal
                              —RP, 7

CHRISTMAS,
POLITICALLY INTERPRETED

When the angels had left them and gone into heaven, the
shepherds said to one another, "Let us go now to Bethlehem and see this thing that has taken place, which the
Lord has made known to us." So they went with haste and
found Mary and Joseph, and the child lying in the manger.
When they saw this, they made known what had been told
them about this child; and all who heard it were amazed
at what the shepherds told them. But Mary treasured all
these words and pondered them in her heart. The shepherds returned, glorifying God for all they had heard and
seen, as it had been told them. (Luke 2:15–20)

The Christmas narrative for me is a classical example of the
productivity of sociohistorical biblical interpretation. Therefore
I want to represent my story here with this story. For many
years I was so disgusted by the commercialization that this
fragment of religious tradition has endured, so sickened by the

terror of consumption, the pressures of buying, giving, and eating, that I did not want even to think of Luke 2. The violent context in which we live had blocked the light of the text, which seemed to me hopelessly instrumentalized for lies. Neither the historical critical method nor an aesthetics shaped by the middle class of the nineteenth century helped me. The baby in the manger was embarrassing, like rich almond candy.

The escape of the yuppies — to run away and have a few beautiful days without fuss — was not available to me for family reasons. Instead we attempted to work in the context, to locate the stable in a homeless shelter in Cologne-Mülheim and to find the shepherds again among marginalized youths and vagabonds. They told the story in their way and thereby contributed to our liberation. The text itself remained a piece from the museum. That changed at the end of the seventies, when I learned something historically that had not occurred to me in study and exegesis.

I understood rather late what the tyranny of the *Imperium romanum* really meant for the people in the subjugated provinces. Up to this moment I held unsuspectingly to my humanist illusions about the *pax romana*. I regarded it as a kind of constitutional state with a cosmopolitan trading system and grandiose architecture. I had learned to read history only with the eyes of the victor. That the *pax Christi* was intended precisely for those who could expect nothing from the *pax romana* gave me a new key to the Christmas narrative and to the whole New Testament. How and under what conditions had people lived then in Galilee? Why had I never noticed the number of sick who appear in the Gospels? Who or what made them sick? Political oppression, legal degradation, economic plunder, and religious neutrality in the scope of the *religio licita* ("permitted religion") were realities that the writer Luke kept in view in his story, which is so sublime and yet so focused on the center of all conceivable power. At last I saw the *imperium* from the perspective of those dominated by it. I recognized torturers and informers behind the coercive measure, "All went...to be registered" (v. 3). Finally I comprehended the peace of the angels "on earth" and not only in the souls of individual people. I understood for the first time the propaganda terms of the Roman writers who spoke of *pax* and *jus* when they really meant grain prices and militarization of the earth known at that time. (All this can be confirmed by research today.)

Of course, my rereading was politically colored. I too was surrounded by propaganda (freedom and democracy). While I heard the boot of the empire crush everything in its way in the narrative from Bethlehem to Golgotha, I saw the carpet bombings in the poor districts of San Salvador right behind the glittering displays on Fifth Avenue in New York. The sociohistorical interpretation of biblical texts does not arise out of the abstraction of researchers who believe themselves neutral. It arises among people capable of suffering and compassion, who search for the causes of misery. In Paul these causes are called the reign of sin. Without understanding this *imperium* in its economic and ecological power of death, we also cannot see the light of Christmas shine. Living in the pretended social market economy, we do not even seem to need this light!

Whoever wants to proclaim something about this light has to free the stifled longing of people. Sociohistorical interpretation that takes seriously concrete everyday human cares and does not make the dying of children from hunger and neglect into a negligible quantity is helpful in this regard. By showing the organized violence — three billion German marks for the most massive deployment of military power since the Second World War — it deepens our yearning for true peace, which can have no other foundation than economic and ecological justice. This fundamental work of naming the alternative to the *pax romana* and to the model of present-day Germany is the task of the churches at Christmas.

Our text (verses 15–20) refers to the praxis of transmission and proclamation. The frightened shepherds become God's messengers. They organize, make haste, find others, and speak with them. Do we not all want to become shepherds and catch sight of the angel? I think so. Without the perspective of the poor, we see nothing, not even an angel. When we approach the poor, our values and goals change. The child appears in many other children. Mary also seeks sanctuary among us. Because the angels sing, the shepherds rise, leave their fears behind, and set out for Bethlehem, wherever it is situated these days. The historic new beginning of 1990 [German reunification] does not represent the definitive farewell to the utopias, to spiritless life without angels, in which the poor shepherds are finally made invisible. On the contrary, we can now take the side of the poor without false compassion or distraction; we can become shepherds and hear the angels sing.

> Glory to God in the highest heaven,
> and on earth peace among those whom God favors!
> — EH, 74–77

FORGIVENESS, POLITICALLY INTERPRETED

It is always the sins of my nation, my race, and my class (the bourgeois property holders) that Jesus Christ exposes and on account of which he accuses us. He asks what we have done or failed to do for the least of his brothers, and in the face of this question we discover the connection between incapacity and weakness, between hopelessness and blindness. But how can this connection be broken? How can powerlessness be overcome?

As soon as we stop viewing sin simply as a private matter that happens primarily between individuals, within a family, or even among the personal relations at one's place of work, and begin to understand it as an essentially political and social concept, then the question of the forgiveness of sins is also extended into another dimension and is beset with difficulties that cannot be resolved in traditional theological language. A lucid awareness of the social situation is at the same time knowledge that cripples man, who is not born in isolation and who feels as though he has been auctioned off to the situation. His sensitivity for the suffering of another has been sharpened, but so has the feeling of having no way out and of inescapable entanglement and collaboration. Therefore it is preferable to deny the possibility of transformation, and a kind of reverse asceticism, which purges itself of work, achievement, consumption, and success, takes the place of an active repentance that could tackle the compromising conditions themselves. Surely in the private sector, the sphere of apparent freedom, we find sympathetic friends who suffer from similar social causes, but in the world of work the total isolation that is built into the system and destroys every attempt at a new beginning is far more prevalent.

Modern capitalism offers the sensitized man a profusion of possibilities for escaping the consequences of his awareness and settling down — though crippled and sold out — in the more comfortable world. Mere knowledge of causes and of their theoretical potential for transformation by no means provides an escape from powerlessness. Even that which becomes intellectually transparent releases no power for real change. What is missing is faith in the possibility of a new beginning, and many find themselves in the position of Nicodemus, who thought it impossible for a man "to be born anew" (John 3), although he had already discovered the necessity of a new birth....

Is there a way out of this situation of powerlessness? Can even the sins of collaboration and apathy be forgiven? And if so, how, in view of the fact that we continue to collaborate and still regard the old residence as our own? Forgiveness of sins could be a reality only where men break the enslavement to their powerlessness and then are liberated — not as promised by some magical expectation, because that merely replaces one form of bondage with another, but in such a way that we are able to believe in liberation and begin to realize it with one another. But where should this forgiveness, this new beginning, come from if society isolates the individual in all essential problems and in fact knows no forgiveness?

The difficulty of believing in forgiveness in the sense of a new beginning has a parallel in our method of production: increasingly, all products are intentionally designed and manufactured to wear out and be thrown away. Defective products are not repaired, but are consigned to the junk heap. In this industrial situation the acceptance of imperfection, the endeavor to rebuild the damaged article and to give it another chance, is technologically obsolete. The "bruised reed" that is not broken and the dimly burning wick that is not extinguished (Isa. 42:3) become meaningless images under modern conditions of production: the bruised reed is useless junk and the dimly burning wick is replaced. To restore it would be an error and a stupid blunder....

The traditional Christian answer to this question [concerning the "source of the inspiration to begin anew"] is that God forgives men. Whatever we do to others or fail to do should be forgiven by God. It is precisely where those whom we have offended are no longer able to speak that God should step in and forgive in their place. But this traditional view becomes a real problem as soon as we draw forgiveness and sin out of their privatistic reduction and return them once more to concrete social questions.

The fate of ex-Nazis in Germany illustrates how impossible it is to get rid of one's own acknowledged past. Error and guilt cannot be atoned publicly since there are no courts and reference groups for that purpose. The public in a democracy is founded on discussion, argument, and control. In the strict sense of the word, however, there is no argument for the forgiveness of sin any more than, for example, the repentance felt by a man like Albert Speer, Hitler's armaments minister, is controllable and can be subject to objective criteria of examination. His associates must believe his repentance. What is required is a judgment in favor of the guilty, an advance of trust in him that establishes the possibility of a new beginning. But even this judgment can be made only by individuals in our society. Family and perhaps friends can accept the one who has become guilty, but surely it is demanding too much of one's fellow laborers that they should receive the ex-convict. Usually the facts of the case are kept secret from them. There are in our society no courts that review life sentences and make it possible for men to begin anew as was the case earlier in Christian culture. Former Nazis, even those who were less prominent, rarely have any possibilities left, other than private acceptance, especially when they develop a sense of guilt and believe they have gambled away the right to rehabilitation or a career. Society takes revenge on those who do not belittle their role and gloss over their conduct; it hardly knows rehabilitation and certainly not the forgiveness of sin.

In socialist countries accusation and defense, self-criticism and expulsion from the party, expiation, punishment, and re-incorporation into the group take place in the collectives and therefore among men who work with each other. Instruments have been created in those societies similar to those of ancient cloisters, which make possible a new beginning for the way-ward and the guilty. It is widely known that these instruments are used almost exclusively for brainwashing, so that it is dif-ficult for us to recognize in them the old structures of sin, repentance, absolution, and penance. Conversion that is depen-dent upon a specific human group can be agonizing and quite legalistic. But in a society that knows only stifling silence for the guilty outside of the legal process, these tendencies of the social-ists appear to me worthy of consideration. In our society guilt remains unatoned, which means that forgiveness is impossible.

What does the appeal to God accomplish here? In other words, can God — independently of whatever "the world," and therefore society, does or fails to do — bestow forgiveness di-rectly on a penitent man and make possible a new beginning for him? What does the word God mean in the above-mentioned radio broadcast, "God Forgives, Not the Public"? Is forgive-ness possible apart from the one who has been offended? Is it conceivable that God forgives behind the back of those whom it properly concerns? In the Sermon on the Mount the man who wanted to swindle forgiveness by entering the temple and bringing his offering to the altar, thus turning directly to God, is admonished: "Leave your gift there before the altar and go; first be reconciled to your brother and then come and offer your gift" (Matt. 5:24). What kind of role could conceivably be played by a God who acts without mediation? Can he inter-vene "from above" and establish peace where none can exist, because blood and tears and blighted life stand in the way of it?

The difficulty that arises with forgiveness "from above" is not so much metaphysical — the fact that we refer to a source of deliverance grounded outside of the one reality in which we live — as it is historical. When we appeal to forgiveness "from above," we show sublime contempt for men who have been stripped of even the minimal right to offer forgiveness themselves for what may have been done to them. Those who have died in the gas chambers or from starvation cannot forgive. Men who with our help have been cheated of their life, those who have become bitter, the neurotics, the shattered — none of them can forgive. And a God who settles that debt in their stead, who makes arrangements with us at their expense, is not the God of Jesus who signifies the indivisible salvation of all. Salvation always remains privatistic where it appears as forgiveness "from above."

The traditional Christian schema distinguishes the forgiveness given by God from the conversion that we accomplish in the world. When the second part of the schema is excluded, perhaps because the guilty one is too old or too ill, we become dependent on the first and comfort ourselves with the forgiveness of God. But is it actually bestowed directly, without the mediation of other men? Does this notion of forgiveness, which acknowledges an otherworldly power, not throw men even deeper into doubt and fear, and is the process that never comes to completion not fertile ground for neurosis? The isolation of the individual and his attachment to the supernatural God belong together. Perhaps precisely in the Protestant tradition, which has renounced the old instruments and institutionalizations of forgiveness, we have considered the problem too much in terms of extremes — from the point of view of the dying, of guilt for the dead. All too often forgiveness was limited to the moment in which man is assured of the grace of God; and the continuity with the broader dimensions of life, the real social possibilities of liberated man, were unimportant by comparison. The reduction of the individual to subjectivity and of salvation to the private sphere signify a God who is related only to individuals and then only inwardly and secretly. Forgiveness was not so much liberation for new life as deliverance from old guilt, and thus the moment of forgiveness, isolated as it is from the history of men and from their possible future, is necessarily false and destructive. . . .

To experience the forgiveness of sins, we need a group of human beings who make it possible for us to begin afresh; at the very least we need partners who accept us as we are, who have faith in our repentance, who believe we are capable of conversion. In the ancient church this social role was filled by the Christian community, which criticized and absolved the individual. But where do we find comparable groups in the Christian church today? Is there not rather a deep mistrust of giving my neighbor power over my conscience and of allowing the group to exercise the right of judgment over the individual? It is out of the fear of making ourselves dependent on others that we appeal to God as absolute Lord and link our forgiveness and conversion to him alone. But can there be a nonsocial forgiveness? Critics delight in charging that the "theology of neighborliness" is banal because it does not include damnation and judgment, and therefore does not translate the *deus absconditus* into the relations of men with each other. Reflection on a forgiveness that is accomplished here "below" resolves this difficulty: damnation in fact occurs even here, consisting in the total isolation of the individual for whom a new beginning is no longer believed to be a possibility. In Germany those who have become aware of their sin from experiences in the Nazi era have scarcely any chance of conversion if they are alone. They cannot be assured by the forgiveness granted to them, for example, by a pastor, because their consciousness of sin is more serious than could be resolved in our nonobligatory forms of church life.

Conversion is more than forgiveness because it includes the future. Our world obstructs the possibility of conversion, for its principles include the isolation of men from each other and their segregation according to privilege. People live as much as possible in small, intimate units; they organize their work in terms of meaningless and unrelated fragments, and their needs are reduced to those of the consumer. Pressure to achieve, built-in competition, loneliness and inability to communicate, and insistence on privileges are characteristic of a society in which we are not permitted to make a mistake or at least not to admit it. It is a society in which conversion is excluded.

The power of the gospel is manifest in the fact that around itself it crystallizes groups that oppose and annul such forces — at once for themselves, potentially for all. The liberation of all, which is the intention of the gospel, suspends the isolation of modern capitalism. "Jesus wants us to be friends" — thus runs the first sentence in the Catechism of the Community of Isolotto. Thus in the groupings of men established by the gospel the theistic, private meaning of forgiveness of sins will become superfluous, because forgiveness has once again become a possibility in the common life. There is a turning away from isolation and from thoughts of achievement, and the experiences that men have with the gospel of liberation can be talked about.

The difficulty and the future task of a political theology consists in speaking appropriately of the gospel. This does not mean that we could bracket out the "icy stream" (Bloch) of Christian faith, or that we cease to preach the law simply because it is law, or that we cease to point out how sin functions today and what causes it outwardly and inwardly and again outwardly. Without this kind of law there is no gospel, and the difficulty with a new language for the gospel has nothing to do with omitting the law or tempering it a bit. What is involved, however, is giving a political interpretation of the New Being, which I do not enjoy for myself alone; what is involved is giving credibility to the possibility of liberation from oppressive structures; what is involved is the inducement model for becoming truly human. Thus, so it appears to me, theological theory offers less help than the strengthening of faith experienced in the present-day *communio sanctorum.* Helder Camara, Martin Luther King, or Don Mazzi bring liberation to those who see them and hear of them.

That God loves all of us and each and every individual is a universal theological truth, which without translation becomes the universal lie. The translation of this proposition is world-transforming praxis. It needs a degree of concreteness, without which it remains empty. But at the same time this proposition necessarily transcends every concrete manifestation and has neither been exhausted nor rendered invalid in its translations. We have in it a greater claim than is fulfilled at any given time, a deeper want than is satisfied. Thus it focuses our attention on the fact that the concrete reality represented by our own life has begun and still bears the translation of the love of God, which we are. The letter of Christ that we ourselves are is further written (2 Cor. 3:3) and further received and read. There is no other letter capable of replacing the letter of Christ that we are.

—PT, 93–94, 96, 98–102, 104–7

ON HOPE

I am reminded specifically of three "church fathers" who have purged my hope of illusions and rescued it from despair: Paul, Augustine, and Karl Marx. In the classical New Testament passage on hope in Romans 4, Paul talks about Abraham as the

father of the nations. Abraham believed in God and cleaved
to God's promises: "In hope he believed against hope" (Rom.
4:18). The concept of hope is instrumental in Paul's discussion
of justification by faith versus justification by law. He locates
hope in this dialectic. For Paul, hope does not spring from our
deeds or intentions; it precedes them. To the majority of secular
philosophers in Paul's time, hope was regarded not as a virtue
but as a weakness, a weakness attributed to women. Hope was
considered "a temporary illusion for the unwise." Paul gives an
accurate description of these people when he says that the pagans have no hope (Eph. 2:12; 1 Thess. 4:13), for the pagans
are those who have no hope, whatever their religion.

Paul's major dispute was with Jewish law. Paul sees the law
as a dead, frozen, oppressive structure, not as a serious expression of one's religious belief in justification. Instead of being
"the way," which is the original Jewish understanding of the
Torah, the law, according to Paul, is a sterile and empty system of rules that functions as a virtual barrier between God and
God's people. It is not my purpose here to explore all the facets
and ramifications of Paul's controversy with Judaism, but I do
want to state that Paul's polemic against the Jewish law seems
to be a productive misunderstanding of the authentic meaning
of Torah. What Paul calls faith as opposed to law correlates
with the authentic Jewish understanding that lies at the heart of
the Torah. What he calls law we would call in modern terms an
ideology with strict rules of conduct.

To the Protestant Reformation leader Martin Luther, Paul's
law was comparable to the Catholicism of Luther's time, a
belief system of normative rules that eclipsed God. God was
hidden behind the law and secreted especially from the illiter-
ate masses. It was obvious to both Paul and Luther that the law
held out no hope for the hopeless. The law was a demanding
and rewarding system for a certain caste of people, the lay and

religious elite, which excluded the vast majority and made God inaccessible to them. The inaccessibility of God or truth is the mainstay of law in the ideological sense of the word as Paul uses it. This God does not offer hope to the outcast, nor in the long run to anyone....

Faith needs hope which is not an irrelevancy or an illusion. Hope is life's response to life's call. Hope goes against the prolongation of what is given. *Spes contra spem,* hope against hope, means transcendence of the given. Hope does not depend for its existence on what a person may be able to do for herself; it is inseparable from faith in a transcendent power that some call God. And the kind of faith that I am talking about does not necessarily have anything to do with the trappings of institutionalized religion. Those who claim to believe in God but have no hope for the survival of humankind, who further or tolerate the preparation for Armageddon, truly do not believe in God. A God-ideology without hope is not faith. But those who have hope and share it through their lives and deeds truly believe in God whether or not they use religious language and talk about "faith" and "God."

Augustine is another "church father" who made me understand the role of hope. In a remarkable deviation from the teaching of Paul, who contends in 1 Corinthians 13:13 that of the virtues of faith, hope, and love, love is the greatest, Augustine maintains that of these three theological virtues hope is the greatest. According to Augustine, faith only tells us that God is, and love only tells us that God is good, but hope tells us that God will work God's will. From my perspective, God's will is justice for all. But how does God work God's will? How does she do that? Where? With whom? Who are her allies and her co-workers? These are the most important questions for anyone who wants to work in the church today. And as we grapple with these questions it is helpful to remember another Augustinian insight that Hope has two lovely daughters, Anger and Courage — anger so that what cannot be, may not be, and courage so that what must be, will be.

There is finally a third "church father" who sustains my hope against hope — Karl Marx. One of the most important things I have learned from Marx is that any socioeconomic analysis that neither uncovers the contradictions nor identifies the agents of change in a given historical situation is both superficial and deleterious. It is not enough simply to describe what is without consideration for what is yet to be, without regard for the sources of hope. I think that struggle is the source of hope. There is no hope without struggle. There is no hope that drops from heaven through the intervention of God. Hope lies within the struggle. An analysis that is nothing but an analysis serves the maintenance of the status quo. It is not enough to delineate things in a scientific way if that will not change reality. We must work toward the time when the inner contradictions of a system of social injustice become so obvious that they move people from apathy to struggle, from despair to hope. A good analysis has to identify the victims of injustice in a particular social context and ask, How long will they tolerate it? How long will they keep silent? When will they fight back? Who are the bearers of change? What are the objective conditions of struggle and therefore of hope?

Hope lies with those oppressed people who cease tolerating oppression and move to struggle against it. There is no other hope than with those who fight, those who feel oppressed enough and empowered enough to fight to exorcise the oppressor from our midst. There is an apt phrase in German: *Wer sich nicht wehrt, lebt verkehrt* — He or she who doesn't fight back lives wrongly. From a religious standpoint, the person who does not fight back lives wrongly toward God. Those who do not fight back do not believe in love or hope. In my opinion, a group of Christians who call themselves a church are a church only if they fight back. To live in resistance is what is meant by hope against hope. —TWTL, 158–62

CREDO

I believe in god
who did not create an immutable world
a thing incapable of change
who does not govern according to eternal laws
that remain inviolate
or according to a natural order
of rich and poor
of the expert and the ignorant
of rulers and subjects
I believe in god
who willed conflict in life
and wanted us to change the status quo
through our work
through our politics

I believe in jesus christ
who was right when he
like each of us
just another individual who couldn't beat city hall
worked to change the status quo
and was destroyed
looking at him I see
how our intelligence is crippled
our imagination stifled
our efforts wasted

because we do not live as he did
every day I am afraid
that he died in vain
because he is buried in our churches
because we have betrayed his revolution
in our obedience to authority
and our fear of it
I believe in jesus christ
who rises again and again in our lives
so that we will be free
from prejudice and arrogance
from fear and hate
and carry on his revolution
and make way for his kingdom

I believe in the spirit
that jesus brought into the world
in the brotherhood of all nations
I believe it is up to us
what our earth becomes
a vale of tears starvation and tyranny
or a city of god
I believe in a just peace
that can be achieved
in the possibility of a meaningful life
for all people
I believe this world of god's
has a future
amen

—RP, 22–23

3

A Different Language
Poetry and Prayer

The final selection of writings centers on Soelle's call for a "different language." Rather than using the word "theology," which seems to imply that we can ultimately find language or a logos *that reasonably captures the very nature of God, complete with arguments and evidence, Soelle insists that what she does should really be called theopoetry. When we attempt to communicate our experience of God, we do not have adequate language to do so, but the poetic often provides the best means of such communication. Words have become mechanisms of advertising and consuming, rather than ways to share what is at the very heart of our existence. While the "argumentative-reflective" aspects of religious language are important, for they help us to engage critically and ask pointed questions about our ideas of God, it is the "mythic-narrative" arena that Soelle sees as most diminished in our contemporary world. We need stories and poetry to share with others that of God in our world. We should be able to communicate what is most important to us, but doing so requires letting go of success and embracing the vulnerability of our experiences. What is important in our lives is not what "sells" or what provides our fifteen minutes of*

169

*fame, but the everyday life of pain and desire, of relationship
and absurdity, of love and war. Enlightenment language tends
to trivialize the world of myth and confession, insisting that
what cannot be proven is unimportant. Likewise, consumeristic language cares only about the language that convinces the
human economic machine to buy a particular product. Religious language must allow us to express "what it means to love
God above all things" (EH, 85) and it is just such language of
poetry and prayer that is central in Soelle's writings.*

WHAT DO POETRY AND PRAYER
HAVE IN COMMON?

The helplessness and weakness of current religious language is
obvious. Religious discourse appears antiquated, unintelligible,
or at best conventional and without communicative value.
"Merciful?" a female student asked me in a literature seminar.
"Is that a printing error? Does it mean genial? Or friendly?"
I could name many other religious ideas, sin and grace, for
example, which have a reduced meaning in certain everyday
contexts and are unintelligible in their religious significance.

Religious language shares this fate of progressive pauperiza-
tion with human language in general and technical language in
particular. A language is taught and practiced that unites the
highest precision with total desubjectivization, the language of
science, which approaches mathematical abstraction in an ideal
typical way. This language is normative and exercises dominion
over the "pre-"scientific, nonprofessional language of everyday
life, which for its part is impoverished and shallow. The re-
gional dialects with their original riches and wit are replaced
by the standardized language of the mass media. The language
of feelings is exposed to a destructive process of trivialization by

advertising. Scientific language does not nourish or enrich this everyday language and does nothing to oppose this process of trivialization; it remains aloof. Scientific language dominates by forcing people to use its language and no other. In this sense the living space for a human language becomes smaller and more private. The person caught between scientific and everyday language is not assisted by its formulations. What the language of the classicists achieved for a long time and what Brecht attempted in our century, namely, expanding an intermediate area where people can express themselves humanly and holistically, seems more and more difficult.

In this precarious situation, religious language also degenerates into advertising jargon on the one hand ("Give Jesus a try") and abstract theology on the other. Franz Kafka said: "A book must be like an ax in order to break the ice of the soul."

Even "theology" is largely frozen in our context. The word itself has experienced an enormous inflation, which is connected with the scientific expression and the professionalization of theology. The existential character of true theology often perishes in the scientific enterprise, and there is a danger that the handmaid, science, may make herself the ruler of theology.

The language lost to us is not the language of theology but an existential language whose forms include prayer and narrative. Religion is expressed on three different planes: mythic-narrative, religious-confessional, and argumentative-reflective. For example, the phenomenon of human suffering, guilt, privation, and the finiteness of life can be discussed in very different ways. We can narrate the myth of the garden of paradise and the expulsion of the first humans, Adam and Eve. This is a picturesque story that evokes thoughts and feelings without interpretation. Second, we can appropriate subjectively the fate of guilt and hostility and express this religiously in the concept of "sin." Paul Ricoeur emphasized this transition from mythical fate to religious sin. The third kind of speaking is theological-philosophical reflection that seeks to comprehend guilt in the dogma of original sin.

Telling a story, making a confession, and building an idea are very different forms of religious interpretation of the world, which we identify with the words "myth," "religion," and "theology." To the secular mind these intrareligious distinctions are rather meaningless. The three ideas are often used in an indiscriminate and deprecatory way. Mass atheism may be right: It is only a question of different language games with the same theme.

In regard to these three forms of language, the religiocritical tradition of the Enlightenment takes a historicizing position that believes in progress. People believe that an irreversible development from myth to Logos occurs in the course of time and can be stated in concepts. The Logos as the stage of progressive consciousness supersedes myth by reducing it to an idea. But is it true that in the course of time myth, through religion, dies in the Logos? There are good reasons today to deny the thesis of progressive secularization. In spite of enlightened thought, religion has not made itself superfluous; it has not become insignificant for human decisions. We come nearer the truth of religious consciousness, it seems to me, when we regard it as sharing simultaneously in the three forms of religious expression. I would like to propose the following thesis: Contemporary, or postenlightened, theology has to share in all three planes of religious language.

Without the narrative element, which includes retelling myths and narrating particular experiences, theology dries up. At the same time it becomes masculinized into a life-threatening absolute sexism. By this I do not mean only that in this theology women have nothing to say and must be discriminated against in institutions and in writing. I think rather that the theological method of male appropriation of the world leaves out the narrative. It is violated from the beginning in the concept. The sexism of the theology dominant in the church and the university consists not only in the unconscious assumption that humankind is male but also in the complete eradication of the mythic-narrative.

Successful theology has always practiced narration and prayer; it shares in all three planes of religious discourse. It invites myth to return. Its linguistic form, narrative and prayer, is sought, not banished as impure. By the way, this is a criterion of liberation theology, whether black, feminist, or devoted to the poor.

Everywhere there is narration and lament, which is one form of prayer; witnesses and lecturers appear at the great conferences of the *oikumene*. When Domitila, the Bolivian miner's wife, told of the hunger strike of Bolivian housewives, what she did was to relate and to conjure up, to plead and to accuse, to analyze and to reflect. What she said cannot be summarized; prayer and narrative would be barred in this form of communication and would die in its coldness. A new synthesis of myth, religion, and reflection is arising today wherever theology has a liberating character. Myth is not artificially protected from the grip of the Logos, as religious orthodoxy attempted. Rather, it is criticized where it legitimates the rule of people over people in the sense of sexism or racism. Myth is not destroyed when we see its functions in a particular situation.

Nor is myth superfluous in the Logos. Rather, it is asserted, celebrated, and repeated. The strongest testimonies of liberation theology are prayers, liturgies, and worship services that dramatize Christian myth, most importantly the exodus and the resurrection. That can happen only among groups that are intent on changing the world and do not distance themselves in a resigned, academic way from such undertakings. They need

God because the dominant interpretation of "this world" represents a death sentence for the poor. The poor have to become poorer, so that the rich can become richer. It is an illusion to assume that we live in a scientifically surveyable and controllable world that can renounce interpretations such as that of God as justice. Only the rich can comfortably renounce God. The return of myth occurs among those who need its hope.

There is a theology without poetry that through various mechanisms seals itself against the renewal of language. Sentences that are "theopoetic" (envisioning God poetically) are dismissed as "merely literary" and distinguished from the supposedly theological. Dogmatic thought — that is, traditional systems of dogmatics and the uncodified dogmatism that is no longer capable of its own dogmatic formation but is constantly setting up intellectual prohibitions and taboos — serves as a system of protection. The legalism of theology and its institutions is another attempt to protect faith from poetry. In nearly all the disputes between Christians and church administrators, legalist language is used "from above" against original theopoetic declarations; the language of God is not renewed. The most important wall that unpoetic theology has erected against renewal and change is the enslavement of theology to science, in which attempts to crack the ice of the soul are themselves subject to the freezing process. Obviously, critical reason has a place in theology and performs a necessary function against superstition and biblicism. But those who command only the language of science remain ignorant in essential relationships. Today enlightened language is no longer sufficient for the enlightened consciousness, since it cannot articulate specific experiences, for example, absurdity or meaning, alienation or solidarity with all that lives. Its greatest weakness is that it isolates us from myth, religion, and poetry and suffocates our mythic, religious, poetic nature.

Merely rational language is not enough. It is too small for our needs. It explains but does not satisfy. It "enlightens" — even if seldom — but does not warm. It defines, sets limits, criticizes, makes possible distinctions, but the most important work, namely, communication, is not attempted in this language. At best, enlightenment spares the area where we can share life together. At best, the language of enlightenment protects the place and time in which we touch and share together the sanctity of life. It resists the destruction of life. It forbids our making an image, likeness, or ideology of God. This is absolutely necessary. It helps us see that neither "practical constraints" nor the "total market" nor "security" is the ultimate, unquestionable reality to which we can subordinate everything else. The language of enlightenment does not say what it means to love God above all things.

It seems that the question of truth can no longer be raised within the historical world and that it is completely impossible to answer it with the help of science. A new search for myth and religious assurance — in the widest sense of the word — is beginning.

This discussion is new, because the science that should supersede myth no longer bears the burden of explaining and organizing the world, at least not for the most sensitive among us. With the limits of growth, the limits of science and its world responsibility have also become clear to us. In the crisis of science, which, for example, the theologian Rudolf Bultmann, as well as his contemporary Bertolt Brecht, did not perceive, the question of myth is raised again. Is myth, the story of the invasion of divine energies into human reality, necessary for expressing the future or even a hope for the world?

Religious language can teach us to identify our feelings, to know ourselves and make ourselves known. There is a shallowness free of religion that is also directed against poetry.

Language itself, which is full of remembrance, opposes that shallowness. In language we do not only encounter ourselves and express our actuality. We always live in a house of language built by generations before us. Therefore the remembrance of another life and the hope for less destructive methodologies can hardly be eradicated.

The connection between poetic and religious language is clear to me in its opposite: the new speechlessness of a family that no longer eats together. Each takes from the refrigerator what he or she needs, the young watch television up to six hours a day, and there is no conversation anymore.

Our own language is destroyed and corrupted. When a word like "love" is applied to the car, or a word like "purity" to a special detergent, these words have no meaning anymore but are destroyed. All the words that express feelings are damaged for us, including religious language. "Jesus Christ is our Redeemer" — this is ritualized, destroyed language that is dead. There are many people who can no longer say what they want to say or what they expect from life. I believe that writing involves a certain despair of the old language, a certain loathing. Shame is a revolutionary sensation, as Marx said. We must be ashamed how language is chattered and destroyed, how people are destroyed or cannot find themselves at all in what is said. In this shame I am trying to find the language we need. A first presupposition of writing and speaking today is that we resist envelopment by the media and withdraw from their laws. These laws dominate our thinking and destroy our ability to hope or — to speak biblically — to see the world with the eyes of Jesus.

The media under which we live and perceive reality represent a selection, which is always ahead of us and always more powerful than what we "see" ourselves. They incapacitate us and train us to regard our own life as trivial, uninteresting, and unimportant. Living under these coercions, we find that myth, a story interpreting the world in relation to God, is a help. Myth reminds us that our story can also be told differently, that our relationship to the world is different from what the masters of our consciousness believe. A star is not just a celestial body when the people who walked in darkness see "a great light."

The mythic-narrative language of the Bible resists the pressures of the media and criticizes one of their fundamental presuppositions: absolute faith in power and success. One of the communicated messages that we receive from the media is that only success counts. What is not successful now — however true it may be — does not get into the program. The sanctity of life, for which I have tried to plead here, is consistently and mercilessly destroyed in the rituals of consumerism.

The ancient myth is the narration of the fact that life is holy. This holiness has to be dramatized again and again, so that we do not forget it or consider it superfluous. In mythical language we give thanks for the sun, bless the bread, wish one another a safe journey home, and remember that life is a gift, not a possession. The widow with the two pennies is such a dramatization.

What do prayer and poetry have in common? They connect us with our hopes. They take us out of hopeless misery. They remind us of our purpose.

The dangers of all the symbols of the rationalist technical world are evident today at the end of this epoch. Is a turnaround possible in which the poetry banished as merely feminine returns home? Will the "mother tongue of the human family" (G. F. Hamann, 1762) creep into the technological father jargon and heal us? Is language only an instrument of world domination, ultimately an expression of the "will to power," which one could study perfectly in Ronald Reagan's speeches? Theology and poetry, the language of desire and hope, lament and prayer are similarly threatened.

Theology and poetry have more in common today than ever. Both are outcasts; both are regarded as insignificant. In the schools and training institutes, one can refuse to learn these languages. Passive appropriation is still endured; everything that goes beyond the mere reception of a cultural inheritance is questioned. Who then can write poetry and teach prayer? Who would do what poetry and prayer repeatedly attempt, to communicate God, to share God, and to spread the goodness that communicates itself?

In a language world that is governed by consumerism, we can only express ourselves in the categories of possession. Our relation to the world is defined by the most important idols that our culture worships: money and power. This means literally that many people fall into a strange helplessness toward everything that cannot be acquired, managed, purchased, conquered, possessed, controlled, and commercialized. The dominating language of possession, including the divided language of being and a helpless stammering that we know in bereavement, is still the best that those made speechless accomplish.

"The human lives poetically," said Hölderlin, nourished by poetry and prayer. Whenever we escape the language of domination and attempt another language — that is, learn to hear, understand, and speak another language — the linguistic creation, the new development of language, is a source of power and an encouragement that extends far beyond analytical and critical knowledge. I remember how I first heard the maxim, "Gentle water breaks the stone." This saying reminds us of what gentle water has already done, of Brecht's poem about the genesis of the book Tao Te Ching, a word of vision, a sentence that speaks of what the Bible calls the "strength of the weak," a theopoetic sentence, a sentence that does not make a statement about time or answer the obvious question: "When, finally?" The sentence between remembrance and vision reminds me that I will probably die before the stone is broken and the war in which we now live is ended, this war against the poorest of this world, against the creation, and against ourselves. To sing of peace in the midst of war, I believe, was the secret of the people in the New Testament, who trembled under a comparable misanthropic empire and sang their different songs. Thus they "lived poetically" and shared with each other a different language.   —EH, 81–89

WHY CAN'T I SHARE GOD?

To speak about God — that is what I would like to do and where I always fail. That is what I have been attempting for years, in the language of women, in the language of the disenfranchised and of the handicapped, in the language of my tradition that I love, which begins with Isaiah and does not end with the Middle Ages. Yet I almost never succeed in this "God-talk."

I want to recount one of my defeats in this matter, which took place on a day in the late 1980s during a long taxi ride straight through Berlin. The young taxi driver appeared surly and was stubbornly silent. When something came over the radio about a high-ranking military visitor from NATO finally coming to Berlin, the driver commented sarcastically that that was exactly what was needed. I wanted to know whether he now — after the opening of the Berlin Wall — would have to go into the military. As if this question had been the key to his heart, he let loose, saying that no government would bring him to that point again. He had sat around for three years in the National People's Army, for which everything actually always stayed the same anyway

and the people on the top made themselves rich. "Right now they
are raising their per diem allowances again." In every system
the poor people are always the ones who get ripped off — that
had become clear to him. Those on top have only one interest,
and that is to remain on top at any cost. "They want to wreck
everything." It doesn't matter to them when the whole thing here
blows up, the ozone hole; it can't go on this way much longer
anyhow. Human beings — "Don't make me laugh!" — are such
a design failure; it can't take much longer.

At first I tried to intervene and say there were other human
beings who were rising up against injustice and the destruction
of the earth, but he wouldn't listen to any of that. I said I had
worked for years in the peace movement, but he had no interest
in that. I referred to a few young people I know in the east, in
the former German Democratic Republic, who preferred to do
alternative service rather than to go along with everything that
was coming from the top. But he was caught up in a world of
hopelessness and didn't want to know anything about the freedom to decide. To go along or to swim against the stream —
what did either one accomplish? His private situation — his wife
had lost her job, there was no room in any kindergarten for his
child, they were being threatened with a rise in rent and evic-
tion from their apartment — was not the only thing that made
the world so detestable to him. "My earnings aren't bad," he
stated matter-of-factly, but his anger concerning the similarities
of systems (the new surprisingly like the old) combined with his
apocalyptic view of the destruction of the earth to result in what
in the Middle Ages might have been called "hatred of God."

I kept on trying: "Not all people want to continue on as before: I have friends, and we all think much like you do, but we
draw other conclusions. We resist this craving for more death."
But nothing made any impression on him. My last timid attempt went something like this: "You know, I am a Christian,

and I simply don't believe that this is the way it was meant to be; God, you understand, doesn't want it this way." He began to laugh, he laughed loudly with a forced attempt at controlling his laughter. I had to get out, but I still asked him how he had voted. "For the D-Mark," he said bitterly. "And your child?" I asked suddenly, as if a remnant of God must still be hidden somewhere. He shrugged his shoulders.

I have asked myself why I was unable to share God with this person. Why I can't pass on my hope, my strength, my joy, my "despite-everything." There must be something wrong; if God is really God, then God is "that which is most communicable," as Meister Eckhart said. So I don't need to sit silently in a taxi and be embarrassed to utter such a big word. Has it become impossible in our modern age to speak about God? Does every young person who grew up in the former East Germany know that talk about God is nonsense? And is it any different in the western part of Germany? Is there no communicable language for the inner mystery of reality? Has it become impossible to say that something comforts and supports us, that we are not alone with our desires and our longing for another life where we don't have to deal with one another like wolves?

I don't really believe that; I have other experiences also. I meet people who, through their behavior, their manner of dealing with creation and with their neighbors, communicate something about God, even if for understandable reasons they may not use the word "God." It is too sullied, misused, bandied about, and printed on every dollar, which is probably where it belongs. And yet people share with me the strength of God they carry within themselves: their warmth, their readiness to undergo risks, their eyes alert to every flower that still grows through the asphalt.

About which God are we actually speaking?   — TS, 7–9

MY LANGUAGE IS MY WORLD

The loss of expressiveness means being cut off from any kind of transcendence. According to the scheme of things so forcefully presented by television, the young couple whose life finds its expression in consuming, no longer even feel the need for a language to formulate their own pain and their own desires. Life itself is not in any way at stake; in fact its value is simply dependent on how much one can buy and how long one can go on buying at all....

The limitations of my language...are the limitations of my world. The wealth of my language is the wealth which I can experience. The tradition in which I stand has given me a language which interprets my own experience, clarifies it, makes it transparent and enriches it. One of its words, grace, contains a conception of happiness which seemed to be more enticing than what was offered to me otherwise. I found my capacity for wishing respected, my fears dealt with, my need for significance taken infinitely seriously. My capacity for happiness grew with my capacity for speech (and my capacity for pain too, but that belongs in my tradition under the heading of "contrition"). That is why I find consumerism an attack on my human dignity and think that genocide — the word which Pasolini uses for it — is no exaggeration.

Consumerism represents an attack on human dignity unprecedented in human history, which has been economically determined by want and the struggle to survive. I don't want you to get the impression that these questions are the luxury problems of people who have nothing else to worry about. Human dignity can be insulted in different ways. When we say that it is Christ who stands as a poor woman with her children on the fringe of the slums, raking through the rubbish, we can also say that it is Christ who screams in psychosis and tears his face with his nails before they put him in a straitjacket and quieten him down with injections. Human dignity is indivisible. That fact was perhaps never as clear as it is today, in a global culture of dependency. There is a profound connection between the injustice which the citizens of the industrial world commit by means of restrictive tariffs, the international division of labor and the manipulation of the world market, and the West's own psychological misery. The material misery of the third world and the psychological misery of the West belong together, economically, politically, and ecologically — and culturally and psychologically as well. To establish this connection and to make it evident is a theological task for our time. We are all suffering from the same cancer. Human dignity is being insulted in both places, even if in different ways. And in both parts of the world we can see how Christ restores the insulted dignity of men and women and makes them again capable of action and suffering, where they were previously only the passive victims of what was done to them.

The consumer culture brings with it an almost complete destruction of the language in which people were able to communicate with one another. For real communication can come into being only where people can express their needs and wants. But it is at this very point that the most profound disturbance of language is taking place, because our needs are being manipulated. In the barter society everything has its price, as we know. And every need has its material substratum. There is no longer any language for communicating in a convincing way about meaning, faith and struggle, because all our essential or existential needs are hushed up or manipulatively exchanged for something else. In our culture "being" is replaced by "having." In a newspaper I read an advertisement for a heating system, which began with the words: "Warmth for a life." The potential buyers the advertisement appealed to were poor and elderly people whose elemental need really is for warmth. But they are cheated of the fulfillment of this need by having something else foisted on to them instead; and this is the way all advertising goes about things. Our need to be, to be with one another, to communicate, to experience solidarity and human warmth, are first titillated and then turned into needs which can be satisfied by having and buying. Our wish for a different kind of being, for becoming new, for an assurance of significance, is manipulated into a wish to change the objects of our consumerism, to possess something different, to verify and judge ourselves by what we have. Today this manipulation of the mind, this being trained to destroy one's own wishes, no longer comes about through powerful hierarchies in church and religion, but by means of production and advertising. Consumerism is the new religion.   — CL, 62, 64–66

LANGUAGE OF EXPERIENCE

We are afraid to give expression to our experience and to use the kind of language which can do that. We prefer to deny and repress our experience through silence rather than to be fleeced by religion.

For example, I myself have certain qualms about writing this book because I am reluctant to talk about myself. I am afraid of having a religion or of being taken for a religious person. I am afraid of appearing ridiculous. I became aware of how strong these fears are when a team of Dutch television reporters came to interview me. We had agreed to discuss the situation in Vietnam and what we Europeans could do about it. Within a very short time the interviewer steered the conversation to theological matters. The very term "theological" is a defensive term, a technical cover. He began to ask the kind of questions — religious and personal questions — which are not customary in my German homeland. Frankly, I became rather irritated at this turn of conversation and, caught up in the spontaneity of our exchange, I blurted out something I had been thinking about for a long time. What I said was to the effect that one can believe only after one is dead. "How can that be?" one of the interviewers asked. "Have you had this experience?" For a moment I was taken aback. I paused and then said, "Yes, it was in connection with my divorce."

It was not as though I had forgotten all about the camera. I began speaking with the four-man team and together we tried to arrive at a bit of truth, only truth that had been lived and experienced. If it had not been for the cameraman, who became quite involved in the conversation and also began to ask some questions, I would not have been able to do what I did. Our entire upbringing conditions us to repress our real feelings, not to talk about our deepest, most important experiences in such a way that our embarrassment at speaking about ourselves in a personal way comes to us quite naturally. While changing a roll of film the cameraman explained what television is and someday can be. He did it without using the jargon, without sticking to any prepared script, without limiting himself to what was already known and needed only to be put into words, without repeating tried — and tired — formulas that anyone could mouth. He used words such as "life," "mystery," "vision." Above all — and this he emphasized with gestures — he used the word "miracles." "There are miracles," he said. "We have to make room for them." Of course, I was inwardly quite critical of such romantic remarks, yet at the same time his remarks took hold of me. As I spoke with these men I was no longer some kind of an object to which they directed their questions. They were no less embarrassed than I, and they too had to overcome the same qualms I did. We had created a situation in which we could relate to each other in a different way. We discarded our denial of experience and decided to talk to each other in a different way right then and there. It is not easy to reproduce experiences such as these, yet such experiences are indispensable to all of us for they make us really aware of how far removed we are from the so-called normal world, the shattered world of normal communication and normal perception. Our ability to leave no room for miracles and to reject anything that is new or different is one in which we have been exceptionally well trained.

By reducing everything we do to some kind of means to an end, we impose upon ourselves a straitjacket of rigidity and conventionality. Oddly enough, we are not aware of this until at some point or other we break out of the straitjacket. At that very moment I rubbed my eyes in astonishment and realized that I had been dead, that the way I had acted toward other people was empty, devoid of all genuineness, depth, and authenticity. I had been wearing masks, playing out roles, going through the motions. I had thought I could handle this television interview in the same way I was accustomed to doing other things — like ticking off a list. Indeed, I had thought that I could avoid any risk of talking about myself. But it had not occurred to me that not to talk about myself would have made me do something worse — say nothing that was of substance. I had thought that I could talk about religion and theology. But one of the strange things about the language of religion and theology is that it does not permit itself to be used. The reason for this is fairly clear. It is not something neutral, a mere instrumentality. When we use such language simply for the sake of using it, the result is sheer nonsense, garbled communication. The language of religion is the vehicle of collective experience and it is meaningful only when it speaks of experience and addresses itself to experience.

Believe me, it was not easy for me to talk about my experience of dying. For me the experience of dying had the effect of tearing to shreds a whole design of life. Everything I had built and hoped for, believed and wanted, had been dashed to pieces. It was as though one who was very, very dear to me bad been taken away by death. But the loss and separation occasioned by a marriage gone on the rocks necessarily involves the matter of guilt. One cannot escape the sense of guilt, of having forgotten or failed to do something, of having made a dreadful mistake that could not be soothed and calmed by some kind of belief in fate. It took me three years to overcome and come to terms with the suicidal thoughts and desires that filled my mind. It seems as though the only hope and desire I had was to die. It was in this state of mind that while on a trip to Belgium I visited a late-Gothic-style church. I realize now that "prayer" is not the right term. I was crying out. I was crying out for help, and the only kind of help I could conceive of or want was that my husband would come back to me, or that I would die and my misery would be over and done with. Then and there the Bible passage came to mind: "My grace is sufficient for you."

For a long time I had a particular dislike for that passage. It had always struck me as a brutal statement that meant that nothing could ever change. Paul had asked God for the health necessary for his work, and God simply slapped this earnest suppliant in the face with that kind of answer. He who had health and strength and smooth going and all manner of good things for countless others had nothing for Paul except a word which not only did nothing for him but actually made his life even more unbearable.

I must have reached the middle of the tunnel of despair at that point. I had not the faintest idea what that theological term "grace" means because it had absolutely nothing to do with the reality of my life. And yet "God" had spoken that word to me. After I left that church I stopped praying for my husband to come back to me, although for a long time I did pray to die. Little by little I began to accept the fact that my husband was going another way — his way. I had reached the end of the line and God had scrapped the first draft of the design for my life. He had not comforted me as a psychologist would comfort me, with assurances that what I had gone through was to be expected. Nor had he offered me any of the placebos society usually prescribes for people in my circumstances. He slapped me in the face, knocked me to the ground. That was not the kind of death I had wanted — or, for that matter, the kind of life I had wanted. It was an entirely different kind of death. Gradually it began to dawn on me that people who believe limp somewhat, as Jacob limped after wrestling with God on the shore of the Jabbok. All of them have died at one time or another. We cannot wish such a death upon another, nor can we spare another from experiencing it by giving some kind of instruction. The experience of faith can be no more vicarious than can the pleasure of physical love. The experience of the sufficiency of grace for life, and the experience that nothing — not even our own death — can separate us from the love of God, are experiences we can recognize only after the fact. Such experiences are not written down and incorporated in drawings and plans which we can examine and check during the course of construction.

Contemporary attempts to restate religion or to state it anew simply do not make sense unless they take into consideration the centrality of experience. Probably it is more proper to speak of "experience" as a concept-symbol, for the attempt to create a precise psychological or social-psychological definition that would allow the concept to become operational is bound to fail. A definition would, of necessity, contradict what is meant, sought, or sensed. Experience sets itself over against the empiricism of normality and the idealization of scientific learning in which the individual is reduced to a number, and over against "bending the knee to the altar of reason."

It would be wrong to think that someone like R. D. Laing, the English psychiatrist, simply because he is important for the religious subculture must be hostile to science and its rationalistic languages. Laing sees experience as more real than the "normal" condition of man, which is one of absurdity, loss of self, and routine participation in crimes such as war and exploitation. The schizophrenic who has "experiences" of an inner world, even though he is not able to organize these experiences and relate them to each other, is superior to the "normal" person who is dead even though he still goes through the motions of living. "I cannot experience what you experience. Nor can you experience what I experience. As human beings we are both invisible. Each is invisible for the other. Experience is the invisibility of one human being for another — we used to call it 'soul.' Experience of the invisibility of one person or another is at the same time more evident than anything else. Only experience is clear." But even this evidence, according to Laing, is destroyed because of the normal process of upbringing that conditions people socially to "regard as normal and healthy the total immersion in the farthermost time and place." The person who is deceived about the experiences of the inner world is crippled also in his capacity for interpersonal experience and perception — and hence enabled to participate as a matter of course in the extermination of other people.

It is characteristic of Laing that at certain points he — almost existentially — departs from the language of scientific learning and starts to talk about I and Thou almost exclusively. He drops the customary net of presupposition, thesis, and argument, and

attempts to use another language — that of experience. Reimar
Lenz has also published some writings that originated from the
experience of the religious subculture and also attempt a new
language.

> It is our experience, arrived at through the use of psyche-
> delic drugs, that the everyday awareness of our civilization
> is only one of several kinds of awareness — a highly
> cultivated form of worry.... The religious underground re-
> mains the locus of spiritual-emotional experimentation in
> which the loss of ego can be tested in the hope of find-
> ing the self.... "God" is the name we give to that voice in
> us which summons us to go beyond ourselves. Proofs of
> God's existence are pointless. The only way in which God
> allows himself to be proved is through the growth of our
> God-consciousness. God does not exist, but we want to go
> to him.

One must be clear about the strangeness of such a statement
in an academic, scientific, political, or ecclesiastical setting. It
gives offense, not a series of arguments; it remains in disconti-
nuity; its language does not inform or establish anything but
rather invites and courts interest. This statement cannot be
understood except in light of certain experiences. It cannot be
communicable as would be the case in the language of scientific
learning but rather, like all mystical texts, contains a certain
esoteric quality. "We have always insisted on seeing for ourselves. No more secondhand goods...." When one compares a
statement such as this with some statement issued by the church
or a theological pronouncement, one sees immediately that the
statements of a normal awareness are completely devoid of experience. Churchly and theological statements are "secondhand
goods," the sole concern of which is to delineate and preserve

a system. Experience is something to be impeded. The openness that could lead to syncretism and self-articulation must be avoided.

We can make the realm of experience the critical question with respect to the statements of religions, theology, and church. To what extent does a statement speak out of experience to experience? Does it express experience and admit experience? To what extent do even biblical and Reformation statements offer us "secondhand goods"? A statement would be Christian only if it expressed our hunger for justice and for participation in the kingdom of God.

But what experience with the inner world is meant? "Immersion into the inner world and inner time is perhaps to be seen simply as an antisocial retreat, a deviation; it is sick, pathological per se, and to an extent discrediting" (Laing). When a religious question comes up in a group discussion it causes the kind of embarrassment and aversion that the mention of sex occasioned among our grandparents. We are ashamed to speak of our desire for a life that is totally fulfilled and unfragmented; we are ashamed and embarrassed to think of it and we dare to express it only in disguised language. To die and to live, to be destroyed and to begin again, to fail and to proceed with a wholly positive attitude — how are we to come to an understanding about the key experiences? What forms are available to us?

To reduce life to the matter of getting things done, all in the name of a practicality by which every thought and deed is either justified or condemned, makes one-dimensional persons of us all. By focusing on purpose it forecloses the possibility of everything that is not functionally productive, such as prayer, poetry, artistic expression, worship. Consistent with this inability to articulate one's aspirations is the acceptance of one other kind of speech that goes beyond everyday speech — namely, the language of scientific learning. Our only alternatives, then, are everyday language or the language of scientific learning. We can either express ourselves in tasteless banalities or we can express ourselves in ways which are scientifically refined but totally devoid of values, while we let language that is human, language that goes beyond the conveying of information to express the whole range of human feelings, disappear. Although thousands have had the same experience as I and have died upon the death or loss of another, there is still no common agreement about what it means. At one time the soul used the language of religion and poesy to express itself. But when society values only what is useful for getting things done and when the only serious communication about what is useful can be effected only in technical language, then the acceptance of this way of thinking destroys every other perception of values. Indeed, it even destroys us down to the point of what we wish for. Moreover, such a way of thinking destroys every kind of living community because the theological or politico-economic advantage of knowledge on the part of those whom the prevailing culture regards as better educated destroys the uncontrolled communication that proceeds not from knowledge but from wishes and concerns. If we continue to move in this direction we will create a clerical system similar to the one we theologians have just left — a system in which knowledge is still power — and we will come not one step closer to Jesus' way, in which the greatest power is in the hands of those who wish more strongly, who act and suffer, whose starting point is not theory but experience.

Reimar Lenz criticizes the everyday consciousness of civilization as a "highly cultivated form of worry" that in the main separates social from spiritual progress — an attitude which believes it can do without self-confirmation and finding meaning and which, along with the established religion, also regards religious needs as something belonging to the past.

"Everyone is enabled and called upon to decide to think each evening, to complete participation, meditation.... " Will this kind of religious experience, which holds a faith in the capacity of man not shared by the major churches and which goes beyond the forms and doctrines of the church, express itself in a way that is socially relevant? Will we learn to share experience with each other? —DBA, 29–37

LIVING LANGUAGE

When you study theology it is important to understand that all our God-language has symbolic character, and thus that there are very different ways of talking about God, so that you really cannot say that God *is* father, as if the two were identical. That means that every symbol that sets itself up as an absolute has to be relativized. God is really greater than our talk about God, greater than any of our languages. We have to be aware of that, because otherwise we will lock ourselves into symbolic prisons....

I think we can learn a great deal from mysticism in our search for a new language that expresses our relationship to God more clearly, less repressively, and with less danger of misunderstanding. Mysticism offers God-symbols without authority or power, thus without a chauvinistic flavor. The recognition of the higher power, the adoration of domination, the denial of one's own strength, have no place in mystical piety. There the relationship of master and slave is often explicitly criticized; more particularly, it is overcome through creative language. Religion, for mystics, is sensitivity, union with the whole; belonging, not subjection. People adore God not because of God's power and glory. Instead, they sink into God's love, which is called ground, or depth, or ocean.

Coming to my last point, I want to say something about changing method in theology, in connection with the search for a new
language. If we speak subjectively instead of trying to objectivize,
we speak differently. If we do not silence the I and its experiences,
if we do not learn to avoid the word "I" in a scholarly paper,
we learn to express ourselves differently and at the same time to
do a different kind of theology. The expulsion of women from
theology not only affects the 51 percent of humanity who have
remained theologically silent in the West, but it also has catastrophic consequences for the other 49 percent — the men — and
for their language. The suppression of the feminine part of the
soul — that is, the subordination of everything that smells like
woman — has done more damage to theologians' language than
anything in the secular world. It is not what comes from outside
that is dangerous, or what is rationalistic or enlightened or otherwise tends to make God superfluous, but rather the destruction
that men have brought on themselves by cutting off women and
cutting out the woman in themselves. This mutilation of men
plays a substantial role in the world of theology.

What took place was a process of purification and at the same
time of impoverishment, when an emphatic, comprehensive, conscious, and integrative language was gradually and increasingly
silenced. What a difference between theological books and the
gospel! What a terrible discrepancy in their very different language! So-called scientific theology is normally an unconscious
speech — that is, it is unaware of emotion, insensible to human
experience, expressing a kind of ghostly neutralism without interests and without invitation, with no desire to be effectual. It is flat
because in most theological language the shadow side of faith,
which is doubt, has no place and is not admitted. But if we never
say anything other than what we think in our heads, and never,
never admit what contrary things we might have in our hearts, our
language remains flat and slick, as theological language mostly

is. If you read male theologians' commentaries — say, on Eve's dialogue with the serpent in Paradise — you can see how sexual curiosity is damned in principle, and how an enormous fear of woman, of this curiosity, of this desire to begin something new, permeates the whole. The basic recurring feeling you get from these theologians is: Who would talk to a snake, anyway? Nobody would ever do such a thing as Eve did! The pervasive sexism of the theology is obvious. This kind of language, which increasingly excludes female participation and engages in a kind of scientizing that I consider extremely dangerous, really ends by destroying the language that theology needs: words that can touch human beings. Such a language grows out of experience and practice and leads us toward becoming different and acting differently.

Scientific theology attains this quality of living language very seldom, and then almost against its own will. It requires a certain talent for subversion for male theologians to achieve this kind of language, one might say in resistance to prescribed canons of scholarship that are oriented to these ideals of neutralism, of nonpartisanship, of freedom from emotion, and whose whole energy is directed to making the subject disappear. The rediscovery of a conscious, subjective language rich in emotion would be an appropriate task for a new theology. It would have to proceed inductively, not deductively, which means to begin with our experiences — not with statements about God, Scripture, dogma, or tradition — but with the daily events in our life that need to be theologically reflected upon, interpreted, and confronted.

An ordinary statement in the newspaper, like "the cosmetic industry was able to increase its sales in this area by 150 percent in recent years," is a piece of news. Doing feminist theology means understanding such a statement in all its dimensions: What really happened to people? Whose interests are being articulated here? What do we learn about life, about the quality of life?

Doing experiential, inductive theology seems to me very important in contrast to the deductivist tendency of previous theology. Feminist faith and theology understand praxis as the first step, theory and theology as a second, reflexive step. It is a general principle of liberation theology, as developed by Gustavo Gutiérrez, that one does not begin with theology but with faith. The traditional relationship of theory and practice has to be reversed. The hierarchical order in which theory or brainwork, mostly created by men, is the finer thing, while praxis is left for the common people, the women, the secretaries, is a destructive division of labor. Feminist theology in its methodology calls on other abilities besides abstraction and synopsis. Its interest is not in creating new dogmas but in narration, in telling. Narrative theology is a methodic expression of this new consciousness, namely, that we understand certain things more clearly, in more dimensions, more really; we get them under our skin when we tell them instead of reducing them, so to speak, to concepts. Therefore this element of narrative is extraordinarily important for the women's movement.

American women have a wordplay about this that scandalizes humanistically educated people: they say that we do not need *his*tory, but *her*story. We also need it when we try to tell the story of God with us, the story of God and her friends.

—WV, 70, 72–74

SUNDER WARUMBE

People are always in search of language for such experiences as those of reverence, devotion, or what Goethe calls the "need to give homage," and the historic religions have offered formulae — otherwise they would never have been able to acquire so much influence over human beings. Obviously, they have not gained their power *only* through lies, deception, subjugation, and clerical domination, but because they had, in substance, something to say and they connected it with just these human needs, which we can summarize as "religious needs."

In a man like Goethe, one who is so free of ties to his own class, to his own nation, who is quite independent in religious questions — precisely in such a man we can clearly see how deeply religiosity was rooted and how it impelled him to this devotion to the world and nature, this Spinozism in his own terms. When Goethe speaks of the Inscrutable that is to be revered, or of the "Vengeance," as he likes to call it, I believe that mystical features are in play. He knows well enough that there is a world of language, but that beyond language something exists that we cannot utter. Goethe spoke on the border between the utterable and the unutterable, a sign of this mystical religiosity. In his conversations with Eckermann, for example, the latter tells him an ornithological story about a robin that fed two wrens that had fallen from their nest. Goethe, deeply touched, says: "If anyone hears that and is not moved, Moses and the prophets cannot help him. That is what I call the omnipresence of God, who has diffused part of his infinite love and implanted it everywhere." That is an expression of faith in creation, in the goodness of creation, in the words that conclude the biblical creation story: "See, everything was very good."

Goethe's devotion to the world was nourished by this faith. Is such a faith still feasible? What would be the preconditions for an answer to the question about the meaning of life that would not only reply, in a Promethean and enlightened manner, with a definition to settle the question, but in Franciscan devotion with the acceptance of a good creation that is meaningful in itself, or, to put it in theological terms, a creation that praises God?

Angelus Silesius, in his *Cherubinic Wanderer,* shaped one type of condensed mystical response. He adopts the image of the rose, mystical symbol of the blood of Christ. In a similar couplet Johannes Scheffler expressed the symbolic content of the rose:

> The rose which here on earth is now perceived by me,
> Has blossomed thus in God from all eternity

In the visual arts the symbol of the rose is related to the blood of Christ, captured in a bowl and transformed in the sacrament, or else the rose directly symbolizes Christ's wounds. The statement that the rose has bloomed "in God forever" means that the Word, the Logos, Christ, was with God from all eternity (Prologue to John's Gospel). But this dogmatic interpretation is, of course, not all. The verse also speaks out of a spirituality of creation that is distinctive for the mystics. To "see" the rose — in the sense of the Johannine *idou* ("see for yourself!") — means to experience the presence of God here and now, to perceive God with external sight as love here present. A natural event, a botanical species, communicates God.

The finite is quite capable of comprehending the infinite. Nature is a book in which we can read; it is not closed or hostile. It is no neutral object to be made use of, instead, it is a mirror in which we recognize ourselves, a reflection of the Life that communicates itself. What does the rose tell us?

> The rose hath no why; it blooms because it blooms,
> It noteth not itself, asks not if it be seen.

In this couplet Angelus Silesius summarizes his answer to the question of the meaning of life. Whereas we ordinarily think we are more than a rose, belonging to a higher order of being, he makes the rose the fundamental image and exemplar of true being. It is without purpose, not there for some other reason, not for use, but meaningful in itself. "For what is beautiful appears holy in itself," as Eduard Morike says in "On a Lamp." Being is not a means to something else; it is justified in itself. It requires no recognition from outside that would bestow value on it; the rose "asks not if it be seen." Nor has it any need of the dividedness of self-reflection in an observing subject and an observed object; it does not need to take note of itself. Wholeness and unity are essential features of this creature.

The concept of being "without a why" stems from Meister Eckhart; being *sunder warumbe* is for Eckhart a description of essential being, of the "innermost ground" in which purposes, even religious ones like eternal blessedness, have no further part to play and in which the dividedness that is characteristic of evil, which is disunited with itself, is abandoned.

In a famous passage, Eckhart wrote in clarification of the *sunder warumbe*:

> If anyone were to ask life over a thousand years, "Why are you alive?" the only reply could be: "I live so that I may live." This happens because life lives from its own foundation and rises out of itself. Therefore it lives without a reason so that it lives for itself. Whoever asked a truthful person who accomplishes deeds from his or her own foundation, "Why do you accomplish your deeds?" that person, if he or she were to reply correctly, would say only: "I accomplish so that I can accomplish." God begins where the creature comes to an end. Now God longs for nothing from you more than that you should emerge from yourself in accord with your being as a creature, and that you should admit God within yourself.

I want to emphasize this last point through an experience of my own. For many years I have been engaged in the peace movement, and the question that is asked me most often in this connection is, of course, the one about success: What is the point of it all? "You won't change anything anyway!" is the form in which I most often meet Eckhart's question, "Why do you accomplish your deeds?" It has become more and more clear to me that in the face of a certain cynicism, which can be objective or even subjective, arguments in favor of certain ways of acting are simply no use. A normal, working journalist, who has nothing in his or her head beyond the questions, "What do you get for that, who pays you?" and "What will you achieve by doing that?" can have nothing more than sympathy, at best, for such a hopeless undertaking as the struggle for more justice and peace; our next defeat is certain. Any thinking that is oriented solely toward success is essentially cynical.

But the rose has no why, and one has to do some things *sunder warumbe,* even when they meet with no success now. There is an inner strength of being-at-peace that cannot make the goal orientation of action the measure of all things. All non-violent action in a violent world participates, in this sense, in the "without a why" of the rose.... — WV, 38–41

LEARNING TO PRAY

What does it mean to travel with the "divine contraband"? When liberation theology speaks of mysticism of "wide-open eyes," it repudiates the withdrawal from the world that is traditionally symbolized in the closing of the eyes. This does not imply that the divinity can now be seen bodily, or that God's only true name has been made known. Mystics cannot photograph God, just as theologians cannot prove that God is. Body and reason are equally helpless. The darkness or the silence of God cannot be taken up into an alleged immediacy. One may sooner speak perhaps of a "mediated immediacy" or in terms of paradoxes such as those of Pedro Casaldáliga when he calls out to Christ:

My strength and my failing are you.
My inheritance and my poverty,
my war and my peace,
the judge of my poor tears,
the cause of my hope.

Thus, what mystics call "becoming at one" is never a possession that cannot be lost. What really happens in mystical union is not a new vision of God but a different relationship to the world — one that has borrowed the eyes of God. God is no private affair for a few who are naive enough or who are blessed with a fortunate disposition.

I want to go back again to the testimony of a medieval woman mystic who helped me understand being at one in a new and different way, in the sense of a contemporary liberation theology. Mechthild von Hackeborn from the monastery of Helfta once interpreted the mystical oneness of the soul with God not as an ecstatic-erotic fusion; instead, it is that the soul thus graced learns to make use of "God's senses."

She once begged the Lord to give her something that would always cause her to remember him. Thereupon, she received from the Lord this answer: "See, I give you my eyes, that you may see all things with them, and my ears, that you may hear all things with them; my mouth I also give you, so that all you have to say, whether in speech, prayer, or song, you may say through it. I give you my heart, that through it you may think everything and may love me and all things for my sake." In these words God drew this soul entirely into him and united it in such a way that it seemed to her that she saw with God's eyes, and heard with his ears, and spoke with his mouth, and felt that she had no heart than the heart of God. This she was also given to feel on many later occasions. (Buber)

What happens really in the soul's union with God in terms of liberation and of healing? It is an exercise in seeing how God sees, the perception of what is little and unimportant; it is listening to the cry of God's children who are in slavery in Egypt. God calls upon the soul to give away its own ears and eyes and to let itself be given those of God. Only they who hear with other ears can speak with the mouth of God. God sees what elsewhere is rendered invisible and is of no relevance. Who other than God sees the poor and hears their cry? To use "God's senses" does not mean simply turning inward but becoming free for a different way of living life: See what God sees! Hear what God hears! Laugh where God laughs! Cry where God cries!

Part of that also is "to speak with God's mouth." But that implies a different, new, mystical prayer. The exercise in seeing how God sees happens in speaking with God as one speaks with one's friend (Exod. 33:11). If there is a verb for the life of mysticism, it is praying. This superfluous activity, this unproductive waste of time happens *sunder warumbe* (without any why or wherefore). It is as free of ulterior motives as it is indispensable. Prayer is its own end and not a means to obtain a particular goal. The question "what did it achieve?" must fall silent in face of the reality of prayer.

Leonardo Boff (b. 1938), one of the leading Brazilian liberation theologians, tells of meeting a woman who revivified his faith in God and his hope in God's reign. Her fifteen-year-old son, her only child, was on the city's garbage dump, rummaging for their livelihood, when he was killed by the police. His mother, hunched over with inconsolable pain, is like stone; she is no longer able to cry. Boff asked her: "Can you still believe at all in God?" He goes on to tell what he sees and hears. "I will never forget her eyes because I felt God's own gentleness in them; she looked at me and said, 'Me? Why would I not believe in God? For is God not my father? To whom else would

I cling if not to God — and if I could not feel myself in his hand?' " Boff comments on this encounter: "Marx is mistaken. On this final stage, faith is no opiate but radiating liberation, a light that drives away darkness; it is life beyond death." The prayer of the despairing woman is not a means of reversing what has happened. Nor is it an inner psychic discourse that delivers healing as its product. It is a mystical act because it does not regard the ground of the world as an ice-cold silence. The woman's prayer is what it is. It has moved beyond the pervasive assumption about prayers of intercession and supplication, namely, that there is a purpose to be achieved. Unlike the pattern of prayer of some fundamentalists, there is no boasting of how many prayers have been answered. Instead, it creates a presupposition of mysticism for it takes for granted that they who pray have always been heard already. Violence has taken away the dearest the woman had, but death cannot take away the love in which she lives. The Father is with her. Who can separate them?

In such mysticism of prayer, the relationship of domination between God and humans has been transformed into one of love. That is precisely the mystical transformation that happens to prayer of supplication. The feudalistic patriarchal understanding of supplication often starts from the assumption that human beings have to go and knock on God's door and awaken "him" in order to present their petitions. The feudal lord then answers or refuses. If "he" has refused often enough even the most necessary things, the supplicant will go away and perhaps look elsewhere for salvation.

But in the true prayer of different religions, this utilitarian understanding is not the only dimension, not the beginning and the end. Religious language and its culture has always created other forms that embed supplication in lament and thanksgiving, in crying and praising. Even though in supplicatory prayer the human being — in the nominative — is still at the center, in performing mystical prayer the transformed human being replaces the former. It is the human being now who no longer only calls out but has always been called already — the human being in the accusative. The orphaned woman Boff talks about is a being in relationship, as is her God.

Mystics have rarely cultivated the prayer of supplication; they have worked at a relationship based on mutuality. They have known that there is such a thing as delivering the self to a grace that sets us free. This deliverance happens when we speak to God, make our accusations against God, and weep in God, which is, at the same time, to praise God — in spite of everything.

In this act of speaking, the mystery of the world is upheld as speaking and hearing. What Hölderlin expressed in his phrase, "since we are a conversation and can hear one another" is true in genuine prayer. The conversation that we "are" rather than "conduct" perceives us as respondents who are always already addressed. We are not isolated entities who in solitude cry out at the walls of nothingness. We do not produce ourselves; self-production is replaced by gratitude or grace.

The relationship to God also puts an end to the differentiation between active and passive behavior. All mystics have known that these categories are insufficient because all real experiences between human beings, and between God and them, are always both: radical gift, assault, being overwhelmed, and, at the same time, active accepting, opening one's hands, saying yes, drinking in. No more is anyone only acting or being acted upon. An activity that does not know the virtues of passivity, such as being able to wait, patience, letting go of oneself, and placing oneself into another's hands, becomes thoughtless and merciless. Only when I can experience myself also as a passive being can I know that I have not made myself and that from its inception life was goodness. Being called is always also letting oneself be called.

What changes in such a relationship of love is the modern, still dominant concept of autonomy, which prohibits self-deliverance because it implies the acknowledgment of dependence. Mutual dependence is the fundamental model that mysticism has put in place of domination. "I have it from God and God from me" is one of Angelus Silesius's many formulations of this basic understanding of love that cannot be thought of other than as being mutual. "That God is so blessed and lives without desire, he has received from me as I have received it from him." The mutuality signaled here is both dependency and self-deliverance. But can they be without domination and inferiority? To this question love responds with a resounding Yes! The dependency of someone who says to another, "I cannot live without you!" describes not coercion or inferiority, or dependency as sickness but something that elevates my freedom. I grow in the need for one who is different and removes my boundaries. I become more beautiful when I owe my beauty not to myself or my mirrors but to the one who calls me beautiful and whom I need.

Prayer also works in precisely this sense where love reduces domination by knowing itself to be dependent. Prayer is a language of love; whenever it is not, prayer is dispensable. Prayer is petition and teaches us to shape our desires more in accordance with life and together with others; at the same time, it is also delivery of the self into God's grace, but not in obsequiousness. Indeed, we are not self-sufficient. We ought not to exchange the premodern domination of a feudal-lord God for the modern domination of the *Herrenmensch* (the master-human being). It is possible, after all, to think of a different, domination-free model of relationship and to live in it, a model that may have a new chance in the postmodern world.

The basic understanding of the mutual dependency of God and human beings found in mystical religiosity has yet a very different dimension today than in the past. For now the notion of the self-sufficiency and domination of the two-legged creature over all other living beings and the elements, which are treated as mere resources, has grown beyond all imaginable measures. Appropriation, domination, subjugation, and use determine the relation to the world of nature and threaten the whole of life on the little blue planet. More and more people sense today that a different spiritual foundation for the earth's survival and all its inhabitants is necessary.

It is precisely among critical thinkers in the natural sciences that a new attentiveness is emerging to a domination-free, mystical religiosity. It has become clearer and clearer that everything that exists coexists and is bound into a network of relationships that we call interdependence. This approach to creation renders ever more questionable the notion of the absolute domination by our species. The anthropocentrism that today endangers the survival of creation and the multiplicity of its species is hostile to nature. In addition, it is without relation to God in depicting human beings as, according to Descartes, *maîtres et possesseurs de la nature* (masters and owners of nature).

Creation itself is dependent on cooperation and on mutual assistance. Ever since his great "Canto Cósmico" of 1989, Ernesto Cardenal emphasizes in his synthesis of natural science, poetry, and music that this cooperation "has always been present at every biological level and is as old as life itself." To inquire about the origin of cooperation means to inquire about the origin of life itself. In this endeavor, natural scientists discover in ever new ways that it is not the struggle for existence and the survival of the fittest that is the foundation. Instead, commonality and mutual dependency are the basis of evolution.

To entertain desires other than those prescribed is a preparation, a kind of school of prayer that we badly need. A mystical-ecological consciousness knows itself to be woven together with all that exists. All that is can live and survive only in the coexistence of relationships. This coexistence binds us together with the millions of years of evolution and, at the same time, with our grandchildren's drinking water. It cannot be ignored and no one has the right to foreclose on it. Coexistence needs a different world piety.

Mysticism as the future form of religion also relates to this unity of life. As its language, prayer brings the unity that is given with creation into awareness. Into the place of the cancer-like expansion of a few living beings and life-forms there enters the well-being of all. Give and take replaces the winner mentality. Is it possible for love to overcome the illusions of autonomy, self-sufficiency, and the praxis of exclusion? It is amply evident that we will have no chance at all without this mystical dream. To live in it already, now, is the hope of self-aware minorities.

I conclude with a description of such a life that is told by Quakers. In words of beautiful exaggeration yet, at the same time, utter realism, this picture of life speaks of three qualities that are open to everyone:

- boundless happiness

- absolute fearlessness

- constant difficulty

There are human beings who not only hear the "silent cry" which is God, but also make it heard as the music of the world that even to this day fulfills the cosmos and the soul.

—SC, 292–98

PRAYING IS WRESTLING
WITH GOD

Who is this God of Jacob? Who assaults and who blesses? I
have written down the words which appear in the commentaries about the one who struggles there through the night with
Jacob: the stranger, the nighttime visitor, the demon afraid of
the fight, the ghost, the spirit who robs and murders, the aggressor, the enemy. In the rabbinic commentaries there appear
the words "shepherd," "magician," "wise man," or "bandit."
Most interpreters have, to be sure, agreed on "angel," and our
story has entered the visual arts, from Rembrandt to Chagall
and Herbert Falken, as well as literature, under the title "Jacob wrestling with the angel." Jacob's struggle is a contest with
an angel and to that extent holds a middle ground between the
devil and God, taking up traits of both. So once again: Who
assaults Jacob, who blesses him?

> Each of us wrestles with God
> let us stand by that
> even if we are defeated
> and put out of joint
> each of us wrestles with God
> who waits to be used
> A struggle waits for us.

In thinking about being assaulted, I am reminded of my
friend Lore, who lives in Düsseldorf. Perhaps the Rhine bridge
there is a ford over the Jabbok. My friend, an exceptionally
gifted person with an arrestingly bright, clear rational capacity,
was for years the director of a training college. Last summer she
had to endure something that I would like to describe with the
words of our story: someone wrestled with her and assaulted
her defenseless soul.

For months Lore has been in the closed ward of a psychiatric hospital. Many nights she has screamed all night long. She has overturned the carts of cleaning women; she trampled on her glasses — the instrument through which she, in reading, sees the world. She begged me, "Get me out of here." Lore has many and reliable friends. She draws a good pension — but she is as alone as Jacob after he shipped family and possessions — our barricades against unhappiness — ahead of him. She was assaulted, as if the nighttime attacker had sought out my friend in order to show her his power. Her illness broke out anew, by the way, when in the United States her purse with her essential antidepressant medication was stolen.

Assaults, attacks, threats, and the nameless anxieties of the mentally ill — when will the tormentor leave her alone? When will day break? And will she perceive the struggle which is destroying her as a blessing? Is it conceivable for her to hold her ground against the misfortune befalling her, to resist it with so much love of life that it is transformed? "For those who love God," Paul says in the Letter to the Romans, "all things must work for the best" (Rom. 8:28). Everything, really? Including sickness of the soul and the spirit? Including destruction?

Jacob must have believed something like this. Otherwise his strength and his wrestling cannot be explained, and above all not the archaic stipulation which he puts to his attacker. "I will not let go of you unless you give me a portion of your power."

One of the finest aspects of the story in my view is that after Jacob had struggled all night he was in the end not happy to let go of the mysterious guest. He does not let him breathe freely. *Survivre n'est past vivre.* Survival is not sufficient. Jacob wants more; with and in spite of his dislocated hip he wants more than to have just managed to get away. He wants God to be other than God now is. The demon, the one who suffocates people, the God who exacts satisfaction must be different still. What should "wrestling" with God really mean, other than to press God so hard that God becomes God and lives out more than God's dark side?! Stated simply: Jacob loves God! He wants something from God. He does not leave God as God is. He does not let go. He does not let himself be satisfied with reducing God. He does not say, "That's just the way it is with your God; you can forget him."

> Each of us is blessed
> Let us believe in that
> even if we want to give up
> Give us the brazenness to demand more
> Make us hunger after you
> teach us to pray: I will not leave you
> that simply cannot be everything
> A blessing awaits us.

We ask many times about the meaning of prayer. To wrestle with God in order that God might be God is an answer to this question. To pray means to hold before ourselves again and again the black children of South Africa who today are in prison, humiliated, and tortured. To pray means not to exonerate God. "But, my God, they are your children." Created for freedom, little lower than the angels, daughters and sons of life. You cannot simply let them perish. To make intercession means to remind God of those who have every reason to believe themselves forgotten by God. Wrestling, struggling, praying is a process....

I have difficulties with the expression "struggle with prayer" — it sounds unnatural to me — but it has become progressively clearer to me that praying and struggling do belong together. To wrestle with the dark God for the life of a human being in order that this beloved person may not die, that he no longer turn to the bottle or to the needle, that he not be ruined by self-despair — we are all familiar with this. Is it not true that we pray more when we love more? That we throw ourselves into God's path so that God cannot get away, that we "coerce" God, as the jurists express it, that God might finally be God! "Prove your power, Lord Jesus Christ"; do not hide behind proclamations, pronouncements, and promises — these we have known for two thousand years — but speak now and say that your name is love and not terror. Say it in the psychiatric hospital and in Soweto and in Baghdad!

Praying and struggling belong together. Who is the God of Jacob and our God? Who assaults Jacob, and who blesses him? Who comes to us as fate, as disastrous drought, as material constraint, as the stranger, the unknown one who afflicts us? The answer does not lie in theology but rather in the wrestling that we may call prayer or struggle; they amount to the same thing. God assaults us no less than God assaults Jacob. In prayer we present ourselves to the one who assaults us. We are naked; we have sent away that which could protect us. Let yourselves be assaulted by God; do not think that Jabbok lies far away and that other children, not mine, live in Soweto. Everything speaks in favor of struggling with God for God, that God may become visible, that God's sun may rise in us also and we may receive a new name.   — TS, 53–56, 58

ON DIALOGUE

On what basis do we really talk of God? That is one of the questions at issue between orthodoxy and liberalism. Is it at all possible to speak objectively about God, or are there only subjective feelings? The danger of objective statements about God is that they lay claim to an authority outside the world and, often via the concept of "revelation," truths behind which there can be no questioning are established and used for purposes of domination. But the dangers of a purely subjective language are no less; it so isolates our experience that it really cannot be communicated any more. "I can't explain it to you, but that's how I feel" can mark the breaking off of communication. Religion then becomes a kind of private neurosis, each person's own system of signs and understanding. But there is a better method in between objective and subjective claims to the truth, in which both are exposed to the test of experience.

"Experience" is a basic concept in feminist theology. Although it is sometimes exaggerated within the religious women's movement so that there is virtually no subsequent reflection on it, it is fundamental to the critical capacity of women and others who are oppressed, who appeal against a dominant theology, opinion, or ideology on the basis of their own experience. The most important criterion for this concept is intersubjectivity, in other words the communicability of experience. So, again in connection with the question of God it is not a matter of my having this God and your having that God, but of the communication of experiences in which we find ourselves together again. One of the most important tasks of feminist theology is to find a common language for God which practices this sharing. The better method for this is dialogue which can be established beyond authoritarian or subjectivistic claims to truth. What is a dialogue, and what do we understand by the dialogical method? Here I want to mention three conditions of dialogue which are indispensable to the liberation thought of feminists and others.

Dialogue must be free of domination. No pressure may be used. If my answer to a question has consequences for my career, if pressure is exercised, for example by an authority, then there is no freedom from domination.

The second condition is intersubjectivity. The different subjects with their experiences become involved in a process of exchange to which all involved contribute with as little restraint as possible.

Here, thirdly, they take a risk which at the same time is the opportunity for dialogue, namely, the possibility of change. Readiness to allow oneself to be changed on entering a dialogue with the religious tradition is indispensable. It may be that in the dialogue I have to give up things which were dear and familiar to me. And at the same time the dialogue lives by the hope of all involved that they may make their own experience productive for others.   —TG, 177–79

THE RETURN OF MYTH

Can an enlightened person still believe? Why do we need mythical stories and symbols if their contents could today be unlocked and adapted in different ways? What does faith mean, if its essential experiences, such as that of knowing oneself to be sheltered in fundamental trust and of living in an unshakable love toward all creatures, need no religious and mythical language? Is enlightened and commonsense language not sufficient for an enlightened consciousness?

No, a merely rational language is not enough. It is too small for our needs. It explains, but it does not satisfy. It illuminates — although seldom — but it does not warm. It defines, sets limits, criticizes, makes distinctions possible, but the most important thing that we as human beings can do, even and especially with our language, namely, communicate, is not the special purpose of this language. At best, enlightenment leaves us room in which to share life with one another. At best, the language of enlightenment protects the time and place where we touch the holiness of life and impart it to one another. It is a defense against the destruction of that life. It forbids us to make an image or a likeness or an ideology of God — and that is absolutely necessary. It helps us to see that neither the "pressure of circumstances" nor the "total market" nor "security" is the unquestionable final reality to which we may subordinate everything else. But the language of enlightenment does not tell us what it means to love God above all things.

I have to express myself in an immediately religious manner at this point, because we need images and myths in order to name our most important experiences, our fears and desires. This is a risky business, because there is such a crowd of false myths and false religions around us. There is a discussion going on nowadays on the subject of myth, inspired by films, fantasy literature, and the arts, that may well indicate that the end of the European Enlightenment is in sight. Francis Ford Coppola's film *Apocalypse Now* (1979) may serve as a negative example. The historical reality of the Vietnam War was made the basis of an aesthetic remythologizing in this film. The historical reality is that a major power attacked a nation of rice farmers that was trying to free itself from its colonial masters. The mythicizing film shows how some obsessed men — lonely, misunderstood techno-heroes — rush toward a tragic fate in the jungle, to the strains of Wagnerian music! It seems as if the question of truth can no longer be asked within the historical world, and as if it were completely impossible to answer it with the aid of science or scholarship; a new search for myth and (in the broadest sense of the word) religious assurance is beginning.

This discussion is new in the sense that science, which was supposed to replace myth, is no longer able to bear the burden of explaining and shaping the world. Together with the limits of growth, the limits of science and its social responsibility have become visible. In this crisis of science, which neither the theologian Rudolf Bultmann nor his contemporary Bertolt Brecht had anticipated, the question of myth is being posed anew. Is myth, the story of the penetration of divine forces into human reality, necessary to describe the future or even any kind of hope for the world?

In what follows I will not distinguish between myth, religion, and poetry, although this distinction is historically justified. In the present situation, however, it is of no use to us. As a writer I work with theological material as artists work with stone, wire, wood, or other materials. The Bible, the lives of the saints, the history of the church — which essentially means, systematic theological reflection, since the institution has not succeeded, in spite of intense effort in destroying the gospel — these are the materials I need in order to shed some light on a dark and confused context. I will give an example to show clearly how I work.

In Mutlangen, in September 1983, there was a blockade of the installation for mass conflagration that was then being planned and has since been built. It poured rain during the night, and my group crouched, shivering, under a tent cloth. A middle-aged woman rode up on a bicycle and brought us hot tea. She said she was a substitute teacher in a nearby town. She could not make an open commitment to the peace movement, as her sister had done, because she would lose her job. "But since I favor more practical measures anyway, I brought you tea."

I was very happy about this incident. Later on, I tried to express my pleasure to some other people. They listened and found it "very nice." But that was not what I had experienced. I had not been able to explain myself clearly in the language of facts. This woman was one of the "little people": humble in appearance, timid in her movements, disadvantaged in comparison to her sister, constantly in danger of doing something wrong in her job — a damaged person. And yet she rode her bicycle through the night, in the rain, to bring us tea. Finally a story from the New Testament occurred to me: about the widow whom Jesus watched as she dropped "two copper coins" into the treasury (Mark 12:41–44). "This poor widow has put in more than all those who are contributing to the treasury. For they all contributed out of their abundance; but she out of her poverty has put in everything she had, her whole food for today" (12:44).

When I thought of the poor widow in the gospel, I understood the woman in Mutlangen better. I was better able to describe the joy she represented for us. Why should an old story from the Jesus tradition help me to write today? What does mythical-narrative language contribute? Something that, although it is contained in my empirical reality, is usually not visible. I use the gospel, or other religious traditions, to say something that is vital to me. I use myth and mythical speech because I need it. Anything that is not needed is dead. What drives me to need and to use it?

A first precondition of writing and speaking today is that we protect ourselves from the embrace of the media and keep ourselves free from their rules. These rules dominate our thinking and destroy our ability to hope or (to put it in biblical terms) to see the world through Jesus' eyes. We are not in a position to "see" the woman who brings the tea in the night, to "see" in the sense of *idou,* "take a look," as John the evangelist uses the word. The fact that a woman whose name I do not know brings tea during the night to a group of blockaders is not "news." My attitude — in this case, my joy — is not newsworthy. If I tried to tell the story to a newspaperman, he would think I was crazy, sentimental, off the point — in other words, typically feminine. My story is unimportant, it says nothing to him or, he thinks, to most people. It is trivial.

The media under whose sway we live and through which we perceive reality make a selection that is always ahead of us and always more powerful than we can "see." The china that Nancy Reagan purchased in Washington for her husband's inauguration is important; the tea that a woman brings us in Mutlangen is unimportant. Inasmuch as the media make a certain selection between "important" and "trivial" things, they incapacitate us and teach us to regard our own lives as trivial, uninteresting, and inessential. In the face of these compulsions, myth — a story that constantly interprets the world as existing in relationship to God — is a help to us. it recalls for us that our story, also, can be told differently, that we, too, live in another relationship to the world than the lords of our consciousness imagine. "Star" does not always mean a heavenly body when the people that walk in darkness see "a great light."

The mythical-narrative language of the Bible parries the pressures of the media and criticizes one of their fundamental presuppositions, that of absolute faith in power and success. One of the messages we receive from the media (and in the United States, young people now watch television an average of six hours a day) is that only success counts. I want to illustrate that with an experience I have had in recent years in connection with the peace movement.

I have given many interviews to all sorts of media people. It took me a long time before I really understood the mechanisms that controlled the process. I unconsciously assumed that in an interview, the interviewer and the interviewee had a shared interest in getting to the truth. This was a naive assumption. What usually interested the reporter was not the truth — for example, whether it was a question of first-strike or defensive weapons, of anticipating or following an escalation in armaments, of the slaughter of Nicaragua or the protection of the Indians' human rights. The principal interest of the media people is to find out whether the peace movement is successful, whether its representatives — I, for example — project power.

The basic cynicism of the media consists in the arrogance of power that they themselves share. How often have they given us to understand that we are certainly "very nice" but pitifully weak? When I attempt to represent the peace movement in such discussions, I first have to try to break through this barrier of the success mentality within which my opposite number lives, to dissolve this obsession with power so that the question of truth can be approached at all. I have to try to achieve a reversal of the priorities of success versus truth before I can make the subject audible at all.

The compulsion to think in terms of success and power, however, touches not only those who work in the media, but all of us. Our ability to perceive has been disturbed and our feeling for reality trivialized. In a culture that expects all of us to be informed daily and hourly about cat food and hair spray, life is necessarily trivial. What this daily brainwashing produces, and what is consumed at particular times and under particular circumstances (news program, sports, beer) have become, in a new sense of the term, our daily ritual, which has replaced the old myths. Just as the planning of a city neighborhood can give a child the message "Cars are important here; you are not wanted," so our means of communication teach all of us a constant, self-evident contempt for living things, the weak, and those in need of protection. What cannot be sold is worthless. What is not immediately successful can be as true as you like, but it won't make it into the TV programs. And the sacredness of life for which I am here trying to plead is consistently and pitilessly destroyed in the rituals of consumerism.

The old myth is a story about life as sacred. This sacredness has to be dramatized again and again so that we do not forget it or think of it as superfluous. In mythical language we give thanks for the sun, bless bread, wish each other a good trip home, and thus recall that life is a gift, not a possession. The woman who brought us tea and the woman with the two copper coins together represent such a dramatization. The remembered myth helps me to combat trivialization.

As a writer I do not want to spend my whole life with words; at some point I want to get to the Word. Writing means for me that I continue the writing of the Bible, going on with the writing of the Book. I want to find the Word of God, to use an often misunderstood and objectivized traditional expression. I am thinking of the Word of God not in terms of its origins, such as that God spoke to people once upon a time two thousand years ago, but in terms of its goal. The Word of God is the word, spoken or unspoken, that shares life and roots us in the Ground of all life. The Word of God is life-giving, life-sharing — whoever utters it. It is not the author who defines the word, as authoritarian neoorthodox Protestantism thinks, but it is the relationship between speaker and hearer that justifies our determining such a word-event to be Word of God. It liberates: there is no other definition of the Word of God.

Meister Eckhart says: "Yet God says: 'No one is good but God alone.' What is good? That which shares itself. We say that a good person is one who shares him- or herself and is of use to others. Thus a heathen scholar says that a hermit is neither good nor bad in this sense, because he neither shares himself with others nor is useful to them. But God is all-sharing."

How shall I express the fact that the poor woman's tea in that rainy night in Mutlangen was "all-sharing," if I restrict my language to that of explanation, definition, and criticism (in the comprehensive Western understanding of that word)? I need more....

Great theology has always practiced narrative and prayer; it participates in all three levels of religious discourse. This can be traced as far as Barmen (1934) or Stuttgart (1947). To find contrary examples, one need only read the declarations of the German Lutheran church on the peace question nowadays; there one can comprehend the self-destruction practiced by this theology. It is unable to express either the myth or its religious appropriation. It allows itself to be reduced to a rational mode of reflection in which the aptitude for truth has long since been replaced by an aptitude for consensus. It is a language that increasingly excludes narrative and confessional speech; it has cleansed itself of every form of doubt or other emotion, and it uses theological terminology in a purely instrumental manner. It does not express the sacredness of life, but instead acts like a protective mechanism. Not a word transcends the technocratic language game.

Successful theology, on the contrary, invites the return of the myth. Its language form, that of narrative, is sought for, not banned as impure. That is, incidentally, a criterion of liberation theology, whether black, feminist, or from the viewpoint of the poor. . . .

The return of myth is happening among those who need its hope. That is the foundation of what is called, in liberation theology, the teaching office of the poor. From the poor we learn the contrast language of hope.   — WV, 149–56

NEGATION, PARADOX, AND SILENCE

In the tradition of mysticism, there are linguistic elements that are clearly indispensable and occur in the most diverse cultures. I address three highly notable forms of mystical language: negation, paradox, and silence.

The stylistic figure of negation belongs to the experience that is inexpressible in words. It is not this, it is not that, it is not what you already know or have seen or what someone told you before. "No eye has ever seen, no ear has ever heard such joy" is a line of Bach's chorale, *Wachet auf, ruft uns die Stimme*. The writer of that text, Philipp Nicolai (1556–1608), incorporates into that verse, after those negations, an ancient shout of jubilation "io io" — otherwise not known in Protestant hymnody — and thereby melds the language of the cloud of unknowing with a language in which the articulated word no longer has to be present:

> *Des sind wir froh*
> *io io*
> *Ewig in dulci jubilo*
>
> (of that we are glad
> io io
> forevermore in dulci jubilo).

What cannot be named positively can either be left in silence or must be named negatively. The Upanishads state that the self (*Atman*) "is to be described by 'No! No!' only.... Who so calls the Absolute anything in particular, or says that it is this, seems implicitly to shut it off from being that — it is as if he lessened it." The negation of the "this" in the interest of the absoluteness of the absolute is the response to this danger: there is a knowing through unknowing....

In one of his sermons, Meister Eckhart uses the image of a ship. "Whoever can say the most of God speaks the most in the negative. This can be illustrated with the example of a ship. Were I a shipowner and gave a ship to someone who has never seen one, I would say that it is neither of stone nor of straw. That way I would have told him something about that ship." This way of negation (*apophasis* in Greek, *negatio* in Latin) entered Christian mysticism with Dionysius the Areopagite and has become part of its tradition through a long process of historical impact. In the Areopagite's treatise on the heavenly hierarchy (*De caelesti hierarchia* 2, 3) he states concisely that in connection with the divine, negations (*apophaseis*) are true and affirmations (*kataphaseis*) insufficient. This view gave rise to the apophatic tradition. Mystical theology cannot rest contentedly with what is already known and with what has been already, but insufficiently, named. It distinguishes itself from the lower level of sensate knowledge and its "symbolic theology" where, for example, God is called Father. It also distinguishes itself from the middle level of rationality that in reflection speaks of the first cause and proceeds by means of affirmation, kataphatically. The ways of knowing that go beyond the rational have their place in apophatic and mystical theology. It is doubtful, however, whether there can be a radical *via negativa* or whether the mystics' language must always be complemented by the way of affirmation — on account of its contextual embeddedness and linguistic preformation that is becoming more and more apparent today. Apophatic and kataphatic tradition, the true and the insufficient, actually devour each other and remain interdependent. Indeed, all three levels of symbolic, reflexive, and mystical theological-poetic language impoverish themselves when they shut themselves off from one another.

In his mystical theology, Dionysius teaches everything that God is not, clearly delineating himself from both biblical as well as doctrinal statements. "It has no power, it is not power, nor is it light. It does not live nor is it life. It is not a substance, nor is it eternity or time. It cannot be grasped by the understanding since it is neither knowledge nor truth. It is not kingship. It is not wisdom. It is neither one nor oneness, divinity...." Here, Dionysius refers to the quality of divinized humans, which belongs to the domain of relativity. In his radically apophatic manner of speaking, Dionysius also rejects such concepts as goodness or light because, as he maintained, God is utterly beyond everything and above everything and everyone.

The radical nature of this language leads into an abstract negation that denies the possibility of conceptual knowledge. This unknowing does not arise from ignorance; it comes to be after knowledge. It creates an unusual dynamic that forever seeks new concepts, words, and images and then discards them as inadequate. Not only is this so in Dionysius but also in the extensive circle of those whom he influenced and who, in turn, set their mark on the whole of medieval mysticism....

Let me exemplify this knowing through unknowing and, at the same time, point to the path that leads from mystical theology to practical spirituality. The story of the Good Samaritan (Luke 10) can be interpreted mystically in such a way that the question of the knowledge of God becomes its focus. The priest and the Levite, who walk past the man who fell among robbers and was seriously hurt, are pious God-fearing persons. They "know" God and the law of God. They have God the same way that the one who knows has that which is known. They know what God wants them to be and do. They also know where God is to be found, in the scriptures and the cult of the temple. For them, God is mediated through the existing institutions. They have their God — one who is not to be found on the road between Jerusalem and Jericho. What is wrong with this knowledge of God? The problem is not the knowledge of the Torah or the knowledge of the temple. (It is absurd to read an anti-Judaistic meaning into a story of the Jew Jesus, since it could just as well have come from Hillel or another Jewish teacher.) What is false is a knowledge of God that does not allow for any unknowing or any negative theology. Because both actors know that God is "this," they do not see "that." Hence the Good Samaritan is the antifundamentalist story par excellence.

"And so I ask God to rid me of God," Meister Eckhart says. The God who is known and familiar is too small for him. To know God like another object of our cognition means to turn God into something that is usable, at our disposal. There are many places in mystical piety where the call is heard to leave God for God's sake. The priest and the Levite in the Lucan narrative could have heard it. In this sense, they could have learned to leave behind the object of God they were familiar with, in order to find the God who has assumed the form of a poor beaten-up man. To leave God for the sake of God means to relinquish a figure of God, a way of God, a mode or manner of speaking of God.

To give an example typical of our culture, this would mean letting go of the God of childhood, the God of our "home and native land," or the God of one's own family. The fundamentalistic defiance in which the God of childhood is clung to in as literalist a way as possible often gets in the way of living experience. The process of letting go would be a process of annihilation of the self that has evolved, a process that is necessary in order to know God in the unknown. To leave the ego or the I fits consistently into the apophatic tradition. That and nothing else is what the Samaritan is doing in the gospel narrative, and the mystical theologian from Nazareth is recounting nothing different.

Images, comparisons, and parables are found on every level of religious discourse. But it's only mystical language with its attempt to stay close to "lived religion" that time and time again attains to "a glowing, explosive language in contrast to the 'cold' language of theology."

An excellent stylistic medium that explosive language uses is the oxymoron, a deliberate fusing of two contradictory or mutually exclusive concepts into a new unity. One thinks of such expressions as "darklight," "sadjoyous" (Friedrich Hölderlin), "bittersweet," "eloquent silence," "filled emptiness," or "acquired dispossession." The coincidence of substantive or logical contradictions (*coincidentia oppositorum*) comes about when in a single statement words are juxtaposed with each other that are insufficient on their own. This creates the paradox, which is an unexpected assertion that goes counter to general opinion or common knowledge. In terms of philosophy of language, the paradox is an attempt to approach from two opposite directions a factor that cannot be perceived or understood. Other than in dialectics, no synthesis results here nor a reconciliation of polarities. The opposition remains unmediated and cannot be resolved in language. Dionysius's phrase about the "darkness that outshines all resplendence" is a prime example of paradoxical language. Other bold word images are "whispering silence," "fertile desert," "soundless tone," and "silent cry." With the unserviceable means of a logical language that operates chronologically, such images seek to name mystical experiences. In the introduction to *Ecstatic Confessions*, Martin Buber speaks of "the language, which the commotion once laboriously created to be its messenger and handmaiden, and which, since the beginning of its existence, desires eternally the one impossible thing: to set its foot on the neck of the commotion and to become all poem — truths, purity, poem." Paradox is the clearest expression of this desire and this struggle. Buber cites Meister Eckhart, "There I heard without sound, there I saw without light, there I smelled without movement, there I tasted that which was not, there I felt what did not exist. Then my heart became bottomless, my soul loveless, my mind formless and my nature without essence."

In this form of discourse I am not interested in "prescriptive grammatical rules" — such as ineffability and paradox — that permit the identification of experience as mystical. What interests me is the collision of conventional knowledge and its language, including that of science, which is and remains the "messenger and handmaiden" of that knowledge, on the one hand, with the mystical experience that is oriented toward a changed reality, on the other. I wish to proceed neither prescriptively nor merely descriptively. The debate over mystical language has referred to retrospective interpretations that follow the experience, the reflexive interpretations that accompany the experience, and the interwoven linguistic interpretations that precede and form the experience. In his 1978 essay, "Language and Mystical Awareness," Frederick Streng dealt with the "soteriological expectations" to which that other language gives rise. "Another function of language found in mystical language is just as important. It is to evoke a change in the attitudes and mechanisms of apprehension within the mystically adept." The adept themselves are changed in their suffering under the domination of conventional language and in their longing for transformation. . . .

The third specific element of all mystical languages is silence, which is speaking coming to an end and producing at the same time an expanse of silence. In terms of day-to-day experience, two kinds of silence may be distinguished. One is a dull, listless, apathetic silence, a wordlessness arising from poverty, such as exists in cultures of poverty or between people who have nothing to say to one another. But besides this prediscourse silence, there is also a postdiscourse silence that arises from an abundance that transcends language as a means of communication. This silence after speaking does make use of words but only in order to leave them behind. The sought-after mediation is no longer needed; its instrument is laid aside — more accurately, it falls from one's hands because, in the place of mediation, there has emerged a union that no longer requires language as a tool. Being silent together is a higher degree of being together and of oneness. Just as listening to music can bring people together more than words, so too can the spoken — or written — word come closer to its limit, to silence, and fall silent freely or by necessity. Paradox and apophatic discourse are indicative of this "silence arising from abundance." Being cast out of this form of silence is a bitter experience because we then find ourselves thrown back into the apathetic silence of prediscourse and left all alone. . . .

Silence has a double meaning as part of the mystical experience; on the one hand, silence is the ascetic practice of preparation, a kind of fasting from words. On the other, it is the self-expression of the living light. Religious orders and monastic communities built the practice of silence and silent periods into their rules. Some distinguish three grades of attaining quiet: the silence of the mouth, the silence of the mind, and the silence of the will. They based themselves on biblical verses such as "the fruit of righteousness be quietness" (Isa. 32:17 NEB), where the word "quietness" also refers to "peace." Luther translated the verse as follows, "Righteousness will yield eternal quietness and certainty." The crucial clause of the Carmelite rules also derives from Isaiah: "In quietness and in trust shall be your strength" (Isa. 30:15).

Teresa of Avila, who in 1970 was the first woman to be accorded the title of "doctor of the church" by the pope, introduced two hours of silent prayer daily as the most important reform in her small newly founded convents. This silent or "inner" meditation was contested in the world of the Counter-Reformation. For the church authorities, the oral communal prayer in the words of the church's tradition and shaped by its doctrinal knowledge was beyond questioning. That people might pray without moving their lips and without murmuring words appeared strange, even threatening. Ignatius of Loyola, no less, was eyed with mistrust by the Inquisition authorities on account of this "inward praying," which they suspected to be subjectivity and heresy, precisely because of the emotional intensity known to be involved.

In addition to this general suspicion of heresy lodged against the Brothers and Sisters of the Free Spirit and the Alumbrados (*Illuminati*), there also prevailed — as was frequently the case in connection with mystical movements — the sexist ideology that asserted the mental and spiritual inferiority of women. The University of Salamanca was dominated by the school of thought that asserted a woman was by her very nature incapable of silent meditation. Her emotional disposition makes her prone to being easily driven into heresy. For that reason, inward, genuinely spiritual prayer should be left exclusively to the man and to his intellectual lucidity. An erudite theologian could advance upward on the theological ladder of concepts and deductions to genuinely spiritual prayer. Women, who grew up without Latin and often without the skill of reading, would do better to heed the admonitions of clerics and remain within the traditions of oral prayer. They were allowed obedience, but mysticism and the way to the Inner Citadel — the path that Teresa herself showed and lived — were prohibited.

Like her pupil John of the Cross, Teresa endured the conflict between traditionally established norms of discourse and the personal experience of silence. After an extensive struggle she secured a legitimate place for her new endeavor. Christian spirituality gained a new depth in the course of the sixteenth century in these alternate forms of prayer. Eventually the Church of Rome recognized this. The subjectivization that the religious authorities feared occurred in both silence and discourse. Yet the stronger counterforce against mere ego gratification lay precisely in the wordless immersion in which all the soul's powers became silent. In such silence the I relinquished all that is its own. And all believers, not only male clerics, are called to this way of inward prayer.

The language of mysticism includes in itself a silence that learns to listen and risks being submerged in the dark night of the soul. In Teresa's life work of reform, this silence is contextualized within the social resistance that worked for the liberation of women from restriction, tutelage, and mindlessness. In clinging undeterred to her praxis, Teresa showed how a different language could present a different freedom.

Mysticism is not only for especially graced and elect individuals. Women especially did not transfigure their solitude in an elitist manner; they lamented it. Very often, they could not tell of God's presence; instead, they were ridiculed or accused when they spoke of God being present. I sense a similar difficulty in the most important religious movement of our time, the movement for peace, justice, and the integrity of creation. The political powerlessness of those who take part in the conciliar process is so great that their language is not understood: God without weapons is a laughingstock.

When young people maintain "vigils of silence for peace" in the shopping malls of our cities, in the very places where the golden calf is venerated, they make God visible simply by standing in those places. In silence they speak of God's presence. In these new forms of piety, which openly acknowledge and own their lack of power and do not hide inside churches, there is a mystical kernel. It is a silence that follows after information, analysis, and knowledge. It is public and whoever practices this silence must count on being abused. Such silence is evident in the daily defeats God endures that give rise to accounts like this: "my family won't have anything of this; the papers once again failed to report a single word about our action; I am all alone in my workplace and ostracized." And yet, the silence speaks of God's presence. In silence, God is *presente,* as actualized in this Spanish term of liberation theology.   —SC, 65–70, 74–76

THEOPOETRY

When one tries to communicate God, that is, to say something that goes beyond the language of everyday life, one has to search. Unlike many theologians who actually want to do scholarship, my own search does not take the scholarly path. I do not believe that searching that way will lead us on. Instead, I believe that theology is much more an art than a science. It has to understand itself as an attempt to cross the bounds of everyday language, oriented toward art rather than to the abstract, rational, and neutral. Why is it that in the world of the West only theology developed and not theopoetry?

The endeavor to communicate God does not lead me away from reality, or from images to levels of abstraction. I try to think in images and, even more so, in stories, in narratives. In this respect, I have always learned much from Judaism. Often I have experienced what it means to have a discussion with Jewish people. There always comes a point when they interrupt their argumentation and exclaim, accompanied by an inimitable gesture, "Now, I will tell you a story." Jewish interpretation of Scripture works in much the same way; it is not oriented toward doctrinal assertions but toward application, toward wisdom for living.

I have often narrated events in poetry, framing and preserving information that was important to me. The narrative element has a poetic magic for me:

> And I saw a man on 126th Street
> broom in hand
> sweeping eight feet of the street
> Meticulously he removed garbage and dirt
> from a tiny area
> in the midst of a huge expanse
> of garbage and dirt

And I saw a man on 126th Street
sorrow sat on his back
sweeping eight feet of the street
Wear and tear showed on his arms
in a city
where only crazy folk
Find something to hope in

And I saw a man on 126th Street
broom in hand
There are many ways to offer prayer
With a broom in the hand
is one I had hitherto
not seen before

For me, praying and writing poetry, prayer and poem, are not alternatives. The message I wish to pass on is meant to encourage people to learn to speak for themselves. For example, the idea that every human being can pray is for me an enormous affirmation of human creativity. Christianity presupposes that all human beings are poets, namely, that they can pray. That is the same as seeing with the eyes of God. When people try to say with the utmost capacity for truthfulness what really concerns them, they offer prayer and are poets at the same time. To discover this anew, to bring it into reality or to make it known, is one of the goals I pursue in my poems.

When I have spent time with someone and have been touched by particular points in our conversation, I often feel the need to write it down and to reconstruct or clarify it for myself. It is as if I experience the conversation all over again, in a more intense way. It must have something to do with the fact that I like to deepen my relationship with the now, the present. In other words, I seek to live truly now; I don't want to defer life to a future, more joy-filled condition. I want to learn to take what is here now, to see and hear it, which is to say, to live more attentively.... To be attentive also in everyday occurrences and to listen, to inquire, and to interpret attentively in a conversation — this is what makes for a poem.

I experience our language as broken, horribly corrupted.... All words among us that express feelings have sustained serious damage. This is especially true for the language of religion. "Jesus Christ is our redeemer" — this is destroyed, dead language. It means absolutely nothing, no one understands it; it is religious babble that, although available in staggering quantity, no longer says anything. This is what I mean when I say that language is broken.

Let me tell about an opposite incident. My five-year-old granddaughter Johanna came home from kindergarten and said: "What happened to Jesus was very bad; they made him dead with nails through his hands. But then there was Easter, and, ha-ha, he got up again." For that happily spontaneous "ha-ha," I would gladly give away several yards of exegetical literature.

I believe that a good dose of despair about the old language, a portion of disgust, is part of writing. That is a very natural sensation. Shame is a revolutionary sensation, Karl Marx once said. One has to be ashamed of and suffer from the twaddling that goes on, how language is being destroyed, how human beings are being destroyed or cannot recognize themselves anymore in what is being spoken. In such shame, I move toward something in order to find the language that is perhaps already present somewhere. For example, I find much in the language of the Bible; there I find rather than produce. I would not like to live without the Psalms and much less without finding my own psalm, even if it is as short as Johanna's "ha-ha." It is important that people make their own pains clear to themselves, articulate their own questions in a greater depth, and express more accurately that they are ... learning to fly.   — AW, 152–54

Epilogue

Don't Forget the Best

Thirteen years ago, when I became a grandmother for the first time, I had the feeling that this new role — grown by now to include three grandchildren — would surely make growing older easier for me. And I became aware once again that I still wanted to hand on something of what was important for my generation. I do not want my people to forget fascism. Theodor W. Adorno once said, "The very first demand of education is that Auschwitz does not happen once again."

I don't want to let go of this basic feeling, and I cannot do so. To the last I resist that this German event be leveled out, as for example in the *Historikerstreit*. I resist people's now talking as if this event could be relativized through comparison with other peoples who behaved no differently. I find the whole white-washing of the event simply unbearable. It is in this sense that I really struggle against getting older, and I declare: There are things that must not be forgotten! Remembering, collective remembering, is not a luxury but the indispensable key to liberation.

This is something that I, as an older person, wish to pass on: Do not forget! Only they who remember have a future and hope. I see myself as a link in a chain, as a wave in a large wave-pattern; I am not the whole thing, I am a part. Not that I bear the root: The root bears me, as Paul writes in Romans 11:18. That calms me. There is a saying from the German Peasant Wars: "We go home beaten, the grandchildren will fare better." Ernst Bloch liked to quote these words. What is noted here is a connection between remembrance and the future; being beaten and seeing justice defeated are not in vain.

I remember an Irish fairy tale about the terrible trials a person must undergo when courting a prince or princess. "The king's son, who had just become my friend, must clean out a stable that has been manure-filled for 120 years. Every time he throws out one shovelful, three shovelfuls of smelly manure come flying back in through each of the forty wide-open windows."

As I understand it, what is the origin of theology? I believe that it really does take its rise in a stable that reeks of historic injustice. And there we are with our far too small spades, talking to one another. Theology that is truly alive never arises outside of and apart from its situation; it does not drop straight from heaven as "God's Word." Rather, it constitutes itself in the solidarity of those affected.

I continue to understand faith as a mixture of trust and fear, hope and doubt — in the Gospels Jesus called it great or little faith — as life's intensity, the search for the true prince and for the reign of God. A conversation, in the full sense of the word, comes into being when people share together their hunger for spirit in leaden, spiritless times. The satiated have no need to talk to each other.

My life is that of a theological worker who tries to tell something of God's pain and God's joy My language has perhaps become "more pious," but it was not my subjective development alone, as I have tried to describe it here, that has led to this. It was my participation in the worldwide Christian movement toward a Conciliar Process in which justice, peace, and the integrity of creation finally, clearly represent the heart of faith. Theologically speaking, I think I am less alone today than years ago. To be able to say so is a kind of bliss: *¡Gracias a Dios!*

It was 1990 when a German radio station invited a contribution from me for one of its broadcast series; I was to compose a letter to my children and to state "what really counts in life." Grown-ups were to pass on what gave them comfort, what should not be forgotten or become lost. The following little text was my response.

•

Dear Children,

In the sagas and fairy tales I used to tell you years ago, there is a motif of a poor shepherd who one day is led far away by a little gray man, to a mysterious mountain. The mountain bursts open, and inside glisten the most precious treasures. But as the shepherd keeps stuffing his pockets, a voice calls out, "Don't forget the best!" The story goes on that the door crashes shut behind the shepherd, and the treasures in his pockets turn into dust.

I have never understood what "the best" was really supposed to be. Was it perhaps the clump of flowers at the gate of the mountain? Or a homely old lamp like that of Aladdin? Was it perhaps the key with which to get back in? Perhaps the wish to go back and not to forget?

Don't forget the best! All four of you know that the voice of a little gray man enticed me far away from ordinary life into religion, away from "its cultured despisers" and ever closer to something perhaps more Jewish than a dogmatic Christian faith.

Of all the things I would have liked to give you in the midst of the enmity that life shatters you with, this is the most difficult to explain. I can't simply sign my treasures over to you.

To love God with the whole heart, with all one's strength, from one's entire soul — and that in a world that breaks with tradition after tradition — is something I cannot pass on like an inheritance.

My attempts to raise you as Christians had little chance of succeeding; the institution again and again attacked me from behind, the church was and is only rarely worthy of trust. But I am also very conscious of my own lack of credibly living out customs and symbols, of making hymn and prayer part of everyday life. It is as if we parents had no house of religion to offer you to live in but a derelict one.

A visible manifestation of the difficulty that children with vitality have with their parents today is the fact that you, Mirjam, as the youngest, did not become confirmed. Yet you live no farther away from the treasure mountain and perhaps also hear the voice of the little gray man. That may have been the reason why I held back from enticing you into Christianity — the word "educate" is surely quite out of place in this situation.

But — organized religion or not — I *do* wish that you all become a little bit pious. Don't forget the best! I mean, that you praise God sometimes, not always — only the chatterers and the courtiers of God do so — but on occasion, when you are very happy, so that happiness flows by itself into gratitude and you sing "hallelujah" or the great *om* of Indian religion.

On our trips we used to drag you into churches; on one occasion, the church we looked at was awful. I believe it was you, Caroline, who announced dryly, "No God in there." Precisely that is not to be said in your lives; God is to be "in there," at the sea and in the clouds, in the candle, in music, and, of course, in love.

Without grounding in the ground of life, this true joy is not there, and our joy is then focused always on occasions and things. True joy, the joy of life, the happiness of being alive is not the joy that arises because there are strawberries, because school was canceled, or a wonderful visitor had arrived. True joy is without a "why," or as my best friend from the Middle Ages, Meister Eckhart, used to say, *"sunder warumbe"* ("utterly devoid of why").

If I could give you only a little of this *sunder warumbe* joy, strong mother or not, it would already be very much. Then I would readily let go of my unwelcome extra-special wishes, those motherly demands, such as that once in your life you would read Meister Eckhart: I would gladly turn back again into the little gray man and sit in the blue cave among the glistening jewels and call out, "Don't forget the best!"

Your old Mama

— AW, 165–68